What People Are Saying about *Trusted Leader*

"A pivotal guide for today's leader!"

—**John C. Maxwell**, #1 *New York Times* bestselling author and speaker

"I've worked in politics for thirty years and I know at least one thing to be true: If a leader loses trust, they lose everything. Horsager's book provides a must-read road map for any leader who wants to win and keep the trust of people they hope to lead."

—**Nancy Jacobson**, CEO, No Labels

"LEADERSHIP can't happen without TRUST. In *Trusted Leader*, David defines how to accelerate performance at the highest level."

—**Dave Mortensen**, Co-founder & President, Anytime Fitness, LLC

"Trust is a universal connector that transcends geography and culture, and David provides a thoughtful 'how-to' guide that resonates with people around the globe."

—**Karl Hick**, CDO, Takeda Pharmaceuticals

"If you are a leader of anything, *Trusted Leader* will propel you forward!"

—**Verne Harnish**, Founder of Entrepreneurs' Organization (EO) and author of *Scaling Up*

"In *Trusted Leader,* David provides the solid foundation and actionable framework to build trust that leads to real change."

—**Michele Freeman**, Retired Chief, City of Las Vegas Department of Public Safety

"To grow, you MUST have the trust of those you serve and lead. David's book urges you to dust off the lens of self-reflection and answer the question—are you trustworthy? It's the playbook for building authentic, humble, and courageous relationships and how trust is a critical element."

—**Joel Theisen**, CEO/Founder, Lifespark

"I consistently tell our leaders that 'trust is the currency of leadership.' David spells it out in practical and powerful ways."

—**Scott Ridout**, President, Converge

"The Trust Edge program has become an essential component of Penn State Extension's effort to become the premiere Cooperative Extension program in the United States. The 8 Pillars guide our decisions and undergird our efforts to unite our teams that span all sixty-seven counties in Pennsylvania."

—**Dr. Brent Hales**, Associate Dean,
College of Agricultural Sciences,
Penn State University

"Every successful leader needs to create a vision that their team wants to fall in love with, and establish real trust within their team, so as to deliver on that vision. David provides clear and simple steps to build that trust."

—**Paul Martinelli**, President, Empowered Living Community;
Founding past President of the John C. Maxwell Team

"Every leader who is looking to build a strong organizational home needs this book. The 8 Pillars of Trust are the foundation for organizational development."

—**Genevieve Roberts**, National Managing Director, Leadership &
Organizational Development, Gallagher

"Now, more than ever, we need leaders who build trust. *Trusted Leader* is a must-read for leaders in any industry."

—**Samantha Hanson**, CAO, North Memorial Health

"Incorporating trust into our city's mission led to a 30% reduction in turnover. *Trusted Leader* gives the framework for any organization to solve their root issues and see measurable results."

—**David Cameron**, City Administrator,
City of Republic, Missouri

"Leaders are presented with so many opportunities to build and leverage trust, the key is to seize as many as possible. *Trusted Leader* is an insight-filled guide to help leaders do just that."

—**Nathan Weaver**, VP HR & Communications, HB Fuller

"Implementing the framework in *Trusted Leader* will dramatically enhance your leadership, elevate the way you impact others, and provide you a winning edge!"

—**Troy Nix**, Founder & CEO, First Resource, Inc.,
Author of *Eternal Impact*

"David said that 'trust is the currency of relationships.' *Trusted Leader* equips organizations with a clear approach to enhance capabilities at all levels."

—**John Butcher**, CEO, Caribou Coffee

"David Horsager is the global expert on trust and *Trusted Leader* is the new required book for anyone who intends to grow a significant business, team, or movement."

—**Susan Sly**, Entrepreneur and Bestselling Author

"*Trusted Leader* is a fast-paced mix of story and business strategy that will actually lead to organizational growth."

—**David Roth**, President & CEO, Workmatters

"Without trust between our network of relationships nothing positive can be achieved. David Horsager has not only given us a comprehensive understanding of the importance of Trust, he has also given a practical methodology for building it."

—**Kibuga Kariithi**, Chairman, National Oil Corporation
of Kenya (NOCK)

"Engaging, articulate, and compelling. David's direct, illustrative, and powerful approach to the framework of trust sets a clear and concise path on developing and executing trust amidst the complexities of leadership, enabling organizations to thrive at their best. An absolute significant must-read for leaders."

  —**Mary Verstraete**, President, Center for Coaching Excellence

"Trust must be at the center of every organization. This book is both powerful and incredibly relevant."

  —**Mark Urdahl**, CEO, Red Wing Shoes

"Anyone wanting to take their team to the next level must read this book!"

  —**Greg Feasel**, COO, Colorado Rockies

TRUSTED LEADER

TRUSTED LEADER

8 Pillars That Drive Results

DAVID HORSAGER

Berrett–Koehler Publishers, Inc.

Berrett-Koehler Publishers, Inc.
1333 Broadway, Suite 1000
Oakland, CA 94612-1921
Tel: (510) 817-2277
Fax: (510) 817-2278
www.bkconnection.com

ORDERING INFORMATION

Quantity sales. Special discounts are available on quantity purchases by corporations, associations, and others. For details, contact the "Special Sales Department" at the Berrett-Koehler address above.

Individual sales. Berrett-Koehler publications are available through most bookstores. They can also be ordered directly from Berrett-Koehler: Tel: (800) 929-2929; Fax: (802) 864-7626; www.bkconnection.com.

Orders for college textbook/course adoption use. Please contact Berrett-Koehler: Tel: (800) 929-2929; Fax: (802) 864-7626.

Distributed to the U.S. trade and internationally by Penguin Random House Publisher Services.

Berrett-Koehler and the BK logo are registered trademarks of Berrett-Koehler Publishers, Inc.

Printed in Canada

Berrett-Koehler books are printed on long-lasting acid-free paper. When it is available, we choose paper that has been manufactured by environmentally responsible processes. These may include using trees grown in sustainable forests, incorporating recycled paper, minimizing chlorine in bleaching, or recycling the energy produced at the paper mill.

Library of Congress Cataloging-in-Publication Data

Names: Horsager, David, author.
Title: Trusted leader : 8 pillars that drive results / David Horsager.
Description: First edition. | Oakland, CA : Berrett-Koehler Publishers, Inc., 2021. | Includes index.
Identifiers: LCCN 2020051892 | ISBN 9781523092994 (hardcover) | ISBN 9781523093007 (adobe pdf) | ISBN 9781523093014 (epub)
Subjects: LCSH: Leadership. | Success in business. | Trust.
Classification: LCC HD57.7 .H6793 2021 | DDC 658.4/092—dc23
LC record available at https://lccn.loc.gov/2020051892

First Edition

28 27 26 25 24 23 22 21   10 9 8 7 6 5 4 3 2 1

Book producer: BookMatters; copyeditor: Amy Smith Bell; proofer: Janet Reed Blake; indexer: Leonard Rosenbaum; text and cover designer: Heidi Koopman, Purpose Design

To my two core groups of trusted leaders,
Joe, Jason, and Scott,
and
Rory, Jay, and Jason
for making me a better person in work and in life.

"If you are doing leadership alone,
you are doing it wrong."

The #1 question
everyone is asking
about you:

"Can I trust you?"

The Story

The Application

THE
STORY

1
THE DISCOVERY

ETHAN PARKER FINALLY UNDERSTOOD. He blinked, feeling a smile spread across his face, as a puzzle he had been trying to fit together for almost a week finally clicked. The woman sitting across from him leaned back in her deep, brown leather chair with a satisfied look on her face. Her name was Sunny Bonaventure, CEO and owner of The Grove, and she was currently saving Ethan from certain disaster.

"I'm embarrassed to admit this, Sunny," Ethan said, "but I've never thought about trust like this before. I always thought it was something people just had—either they have your trust or they don't; you are a trustworthy person or you aren't. I mean, I know that trust can be gained or lost based on your actions, but I always thought that meant the big things, you know, like malicious dishonesty or breaking a promise."

Sunny nodded. "I think most people understand trust like that. It's normal. We always notice larger betrayals," she explained. "But trust is much more subtle. It can be felt in every interaction, and it's present in every choice. Every single

action you take either increases or decreases trust. There really is no neutral. It took me a while to learn that, after taking over for my father. Once I did, I was able to turn the whole resort around into what it has become today." Behind Sunny was a wall of floor-to-ceiling windows that looked out onto a scene of absolute winter perfection. The peak of an imposing, snow-covered mountain pierced the sky. Sinuous white lines cut through the green of the trees, and the skiers were little black dots racing down the slopes.

Ethan felt two distinct and conflicting emotions. On the one hand, he felt the lightness that comes with profound relief at having finally understood what Sunny had been trying to teach him all week. He was fairly certain that she had just handed him the tools he needed to get his faltering company, 10K Solutions, back on track. But he also felt chagrined, even a little ashamed. Until a week ago, he had been sailing through life, confident in his successes and achievements, thinking he was the world's best leader at the helm of a company about to revolutionize the auto industry. Instead, Ethan now realized he had been woefully naive, blind to what was going on at his own company. As he was learning from Sunny, he realized he had been taking it for granted that everyone on his team trusted in his leadership.

"I've always thought of myself as a trustworthy person," he told Sunny. "I keep my commitments or communicate if I unexpectedly can't. I have integrity, and I've always conducted my business with transparency and honesty." It had never occurred to Ethan that people might not trust him on the basis of that alone. "But I think I finally see what you've been trying to tell me. It's not enough! All the things I think make me a trustworthy person are invisible to other people. How would they know? And if they can't see what makes me trustworthy. . . ." He paused, processing this moment of clarity. "How are they meant to trust me?" Ethan wanted to be sure he was on the right track.

Sunny leaned forward in her chair, sensing Ethan's hesitation. "Most people think of trust like a bank account," she offered. "You honor some commitments, you help people out, you tell the truth, and you think that you are putting trust, like money, into that account. You think that it sits there waiting for you when you need it." Later, she explained, people think they can just go to the trust bank account and "withdraw" their trust currency. "But that's not how it works," Sunny explained. "If you don't continually reinforce trust in any relationship, it will erode and disappear, no matter how much was in your bank account last week, last month, or last year."

Ethan sat up, intrigued. "That's exactly how I thought trust worked," he said. "I just assumed my team, my whole company, would trust me just because I'm the leader." He suddenly felt less enthusiastic. "They must think I'm incredibly arrogant! And even worse—now they don't even trust each other, and I think it's all my fault. It's going to be a long haul to rebuild trust from the ground up. If we even make it that long, of course." A looming deadline was the root of the crisis that had bowled Ethan over like a stampede of elephants the previous week. If 10K Solutions was not able to deliver, the company would be toast before he even got the chance to rebuild his team's trust.

"Not necessarily!" said Sunny, with a reassuring look. "Trust can be built or lost in a moment. Some things do take time, but you can begin to build trust right away if you start taking the right actions." It always comes down to action, she explained. "Making sure that every day you are actively and intentionally taking steps to build and reinforce trust. It's why we have the 8 Pillars I told you about. Without some sort of comprehensive framework to guide you, it's too easy for these things to get lost in the constant grind of everyday tasks."

Ethan had not been totally convinced by the 8 Pillars model when he first heard about it. "It just seemed so broad," he told Sunny. "I mean, isn't eight steps straining the modern attention span? Most corporate models don't go much above five steps." He hoped the levity in his tone came through. He had seen many organizational models throughout his career and had a slight aversion to them. When Sunny said her model had eight different components, Ethan had been skeptical.

"Oh, we are very familiar with that!" Luckily, Sunny appreciated his irreverence and laughed at the quip. "This place was overrun with methods and five-step models when I took over," she said. "My dad seemed to introduce a new one every month. They all had merit, but it was too much, and the sheer number of them just ended up causing more harm than good." But the 8 Pillars model was different. "I don't see the 8 Pillars as a rigid structure to be followed step by step. Their real strength is in their interconnectedness. They work individually to solve problems, but all eight together are what builds systemic trust." As she explained to Ethan: "A trustworthy person and a trustworthy organization are not the same thing. It's perfectly possible to be a trustworthy person but fail to build a trustworthy organization."

It was hard not to feel inspired around Sunny. Maybe there was hope for 10K, Ethan thought, even if their deadline was approaching with terrifying speed. He felt like he had the tools now, and more important, the understanding of how and why things went wrong. When Ethan had arrived at The Grove a week earlier, he'd never expected to be sitting in a stunning library, talking with the owner of a ski resort about trust. A treasure trove of insight about how to bring 10K back from the brink was the last thing he had expected to find in this out-of-the-way ski lodge in Colorado. Planning their annual getaway with his three best friends from college, Ethan had hoped to enjoy the slopes for an extended weekend. Instead, he had arrived at The Grove in a daze, after finding out earlier that morning about a complete breakdown at 10K.

The soft chime of a clock told Sunny and Ethan that it was getting late. Glancing out the window, Sunny saw skiers heading in as the sun was setting. "I'll be crossing my fingers for good news at your appointment with the surgeon tomorrow!" she said, rising from the leather chair. "And we'll be sure to chat at least one more time before you leave." As she approached Ethan, she picked up the crutches he'd leaned against the wall.

Ethan levered himself up on his good leg, trying to keep the one that was strapped down under layers of plastic and Velcro from knocking into anything. "I'm learning so much, Sunny," he said, accepting the crutches, "and I really appreciate all the time you're spending to help me out."

"It's absolutely my pleasure," Sunny replied, "and I have a feeling 10K is going to be just fine!"

The doctor's appointment that Ethan hoped would give him medical clearance to fly home wasn't until tomorrow morning, so he still had plenty of free time on his hands. He decided to sit by the fire that evening in what The Grove called the Great Room, an open space in the middle of the resort. Beautiful rustic furniture provided a comfortable atmosphere for people to chat, sip on beverages, or gaze at the mountain. One family lounged on a scatter of floor cushions playing a board game. He ordered a mug of hot cocoa and spent the rest of the evening writing notes about the afternoon's epiphany on trust.

The Great Room looked out on a picturesque scene through another enormous wall of windows. The mountain was illuminated by the moon and stars with strings of lights hung along the paths and ski lifts. Lamps glowed through the falling snow, resembling fuzzy dandelion tops. Inside, three massive fireplaces crackled merrily. But the most striking feature was a beautiful old Aspen growing straight up through the floor, lending an otherworldly majesty to the space.

If I had to get stuck somewhere, Ethan thought, *I certainly feel lucky it is in a place like this!*

2
MAYDAY, MAYDAY

ONE WEEK EARLIER, ETHAN PARKER, founder and CEO of 10K Solutions, had sailed into his office, feeling good about the future. It was a brisk Minnesota morning in January, which most people would call frigid. Ethan found it invigorating. He'd always loved winter, and his yearly ski trip with his three best friends from college—known as the Brain Trust—was mere hours away. Tomorrow morning they'd hit the slopes for three days of nose-numbing, head-clearing, Colorado mountain air. Ethan loved the speed and couldn't wait to gondolier up those peaks, then feel the adrenaline rush of racing down that mountain, pushing the edge of control.

But life was about to throw him a curve ball of epic proportions. It was the meeting that changed everything. More precisely, it was when Jenna, 10K's COO, had said, *"I have to change my seven to a four."* That one little sentence could bring down much more than Ethan's weekend plans.

He had called a morning strategy meeting with his top executives. Their software release date was May 1, an easy four months away—something they'd been hard at work on for a year now. It was one of many meetings to make sure this project was all sewn up, in the bag, and done on time.

But the atmosphere in the room was tense. There was a distinct lack of post-holiday camaraderie, and everyone sat quietly, greeting each other with just the most basic professional courtesy.

"So," he said, once the team had settled in their seats around the conference table. "First of May. How are we looking?"

The rush to reply was anything but a stampede. No one said a word.

Don't all jump in at once, he was about to say, but he stopped himself. The wooden expressions around the table told him this was not the time for a joke.

"Okaaay . . . ," Ethan said. "Let's do it this way. Scale of one to ten, ten says we coast through without breaking a sweat, one says we flat out don't make it." He looked at his COO. "Jenna? Give me a number."

Jenna hesitated before responding. "Seven," she replied.

Ouch. He'd expected a ten, a nine at worst. That's why he'd called on Jenna first—she was one of the most capable executives he had ever met. A VP by thirty, Jenna was laser-focused and brought a positive, relentless determination to every project she handled.

Ethan looked at Zach, the director of software. You'd never know from his unassuming personality that Zach had started college at sixteen and gotten his master's by twenty-two. "Zach?"

Looking down at the table, Zach slowly replied. "Um . . . eight?"

Ethan would have felt better if Zach hadn't phrased it as a question. "Iris?" he asked in an uneasy tone.

Iris hesitated, looking at her hands in her lap. She was the lead UX designer, in charge of user interface of the finished product. She was silent long enough that a few people shifted uneasily in their chairs. Just as Ethan was about to say something, Iris looked up and took a deep breath, bracing herself.

"Ethan, I have to be honest," she said. "This is really difficult for me to say, but I just can't go higher than a three."

A three? It took a moment for Iris's response to register. *Just barely above "we flat out don't make it"?* Scanning the room and the rest of the team, Ethan noticed that Jenna seemed to have relaxed, and Zach was hesitantly looking around at the other faces. Not knowing what else to do, Ethan cleared his throat and turned toward Dom, chief technology officer, parked at the far end of the conference table.

"Dom?" Ethan hoped for a miracle. Dominick was known for his incredible efficiency. As the person tracking overall design and system integration, his view carried extra weight.

Dom sighed. His frank expression spoke volumes. "I'm going to have to agree with Iris. Give it a three."

This bombshell stunned everyone into silence, which stretched on for several very uncomfortable moments until Jenna spoke. "I'm really sorry, Ethan, but they're right," she said, looking directly at him. "I have to change my seven to a four."

That was the moment it really sank in, the moment Ethan's stomach tightened. The release date was in serious jeopardy, not to mention his weekend plans.

After Iris's revelation, Ethan completed the circuit around the table. No one ventured lower than the apocalyptic three, but there was nothing over a six from the rest. Not a single ten from the group. Still, the worst hit had been from the company optimist, Jenna. *I have to change my seven to a four.* How had his COO not known until now that Iris and Dominick had such serious misgivings about their progress? How had Ethan himself not known? How had his team gone from having things clearly in hand to a situation that justified pure panic?

For the next twenty minutes, Ethan led the group through an ad hoc pep talk, hoping he was offering up more than be-positive platitudes. But as everyone filed out of the conference room, Ethan could feel the tension linger. Jenna was the last to leave.

"Hey Jenna, do you have a minute?" Ethan asked. He wasn't sure if it was anxiety or a need to take action—any action—that made him blurt out the question. Probably a little of both. He just knew he needed to touch base with someone from the team, and as COO, Jenna usually had the pulse of the whole organization.

"Sure," she said, but Ethan could tell Jenna was as eager as everyone else had been to escape.

"I have to say," Ethan began, "I was not expecting this meeting to go so . . . ," he trailed off. *Badly* did not seem an adequate word to express what had just happened. "I feel like I've missed something big if we're this behind. Any, ah, insight?" He was not sure what to say.

Jenna stared ahead, her I-have-it-all-under-control look firmly in place. This attitude could instill confidence in anyone, but today she seemed to be hiding behind a façade of professionalism. "To be perfectly honest," she started, "I was not looking forward to this meeting. Everyone was pretty nervous about it. But we're just not hitting our metrics." She told Ethan that a few divisions had been struggling. "There is some level of communication breakdown, and there is definitely siloing going on. I hate to break it to you, but the problem is company-wide at this point."

Ethan had picked up on some of the departmental distance, but nothing that could have predicted this. Why hadn't anyone come to him before now? Clearly 10K Solutions had a massive communications problem. It had always been Ethan's goal to lead with integrity. How could it be that even his closest colleagues, his leadership team, felt they couldn't come to him with such critical information? Above all, Ethan considered himself to be an open and honest person. How was it possible that his own organization seemed to lack these very same qualities?

The shock and worry he felt must have shown on his face, because Jenna pivoted to a more optimistic tone. "Look, a three is not a one, right?" she said. "You said a one was 'no way to make it' and no one said one. At least we're all on the same page now and we can start to make some changes. I think the team felt good about finally saying what was on their minds."

3
CHOICES

"I'M SO SORRY," Maya said, after Ethan described the catastrophic meeting to his wife. "Do you need me to pick you up? I can cancel my afternoon meeting." He sat in his office, sorting through the wreckage of the morning. Just hearing her voice over the phone made him relax a little, made things seem brighter somehow.

"That's all right," Ethan said. "I can take an Uber home. I have some logistics to wrap up before I leave." He wasn't sure of his next move yet. His mind was going in a thousand directions at once, scrambling to trace where they'd gotten off track. The company had never missed a deadline—not once in seven years! "If we don't deliver on May 1," he told Maya, "the biggest investors might get cold feet and drop out of the project."

Might? Who was he kidding? The investors would pull out, and so would the consortium. Their funding would be gone and so would the majority of their employees. The company would have to close up shop altogether.

"It's not the end of the world," said Maya, reading his mind. "I was already planning to go back to work after I defend my dissertation. After the baby, at least."

Ethan smiled despite himself. Here she was, on the cusp of getting her doctorate, creating a new human, and without batting an eye, she was strategizing about how to help them engineer a financial comeback. That was his Maya, all right.

He gazed out the window. "I'm hoping there is still a way to salvage things. The first question is, how deep does this problem go?" He couldn't really expect to chart a course out of this mess without knowing how and why they'd gotten into it in the first place. Problem was, he didn't have an answer.

"Anyway," he added, "don't miss your class today. I'll call the guys and cancel. I'll let them know they'll have to break their downhill records without me this year." He didn't see another way. "Time to burn the midnight oil."

"You'll figure it out, honey," said Maya. "Give yourself time. Trust yourself. You'll find the thread that weaves it all back together. That's what you do best."

Ethan felt a little better. He figured he'd spend the day getting more detailed feedback from his team and then camp out at the office into the wee hours.

People often assumed that 10K Solutions was a reference to the company's home state of Minnesota, the "Land of 10,000 Lakes." Some who knew Ethan's background figured it was an inside joke, referring to the 10K Nordic ski races he loved so much. Neither of those were the true origin of the company's name, though. In reality, Ethan had been inspired by the ancient Chinese phrase "the ten thousand things," which roughly translates to "too many to count." Finding the thread in the labyrinth, seeing the puzzle pieces as a whole image, that was Ethan's unique gift.

His phone rang and the caller ID showed his friend Pete's name. Ethan winced, knowing he would have to tell everyone about his change in plans. "Ethan!" came his's friend's enthusiastic voice. "You all set for some powder? The forecast is looking great!"

Fresh thoughts of cold, crisp mountain air and the anticipation of that first run down the slope flashed through Ethan's mind. Connecting with his friends on their annual ski trip was how he reset and cleared his head. He looked forward to it all year.

"I've got some bad news," Ethan said, sighing. "I'm going to have to cancel. Some things have gone south here and it's all hands on deck. I'm really sorry to be last minute about it."

"Aw, dude, are you sure?" said Pete, switching to persuasion. "It's just the weekend! You'll be back bright and early on Monday!"

Ethan felt terrible. "I know, it's killing me, but I really don't think I can." He tried to explain about the looming deadline. "I don't know what happened, but things are a royal catastrophe here. I'd feel like a captain abandoning ship, and I don't really have time to spare."

"Hey, how about this," said Pete. "Friday night, after a day on the slopes, the four of us sit down, take the whole situation apart, and brainstorm over a massive feast. We're all entrepreneurs, right? It will be like a strategy consult with your own personal advisory board!"

Ethan was touched, and tempted. This weekend was their only chance to catch up all year—would his friends really want to spend it focused on his business problems? But he knew he didn't even need to ask. The four had been friends for over twenty years and never missed a beat. They were always there for over each other. He knew where they stood, and he always knew he could count on them.

The promise Ethan had just made to his team about turning things around tugged at him, but Pete had a good point. The mere idea of brainstorming with his old friends lifted at least some of the gloomy weight from his shoulders. Ethan smiled. "Tempting, this is very tempting."

"Right," commanded Pete. "So you are going to pack up, go home, grab your gear, and meet us on the mountain. I'll see you there!" And without giving Ethan a chance to respond, the call disconnected.

The idea was tempting indeed. And it really was just the weekend. Ethan would be back on Monday no matter what, perhaps with some new insights about what had gone wrong. With the baby coming so soon, he also knew this might be his last chance to go skiing for a long time.

His mind made up, Ethan grabbed his jacket, gave a last, slightly guilty look around his office, and headed toward the parking lot.

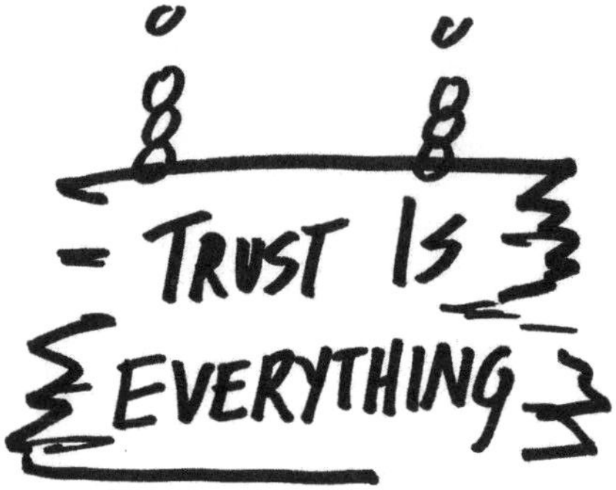
TRUST IS
EVERYTHING

4
THE BRAIN TRUST

ETHAN WAS THE FIRST to arrive at The Grove, a small ski resort that was decidedly off the beaten path. The Brain Trust had a few regular spots, but this year the group was trying something new. On the long car ride from the airport, Ethan tried to convince himself that he had made the right call. A few days of skiing in the crisp alpine air, taking in those majestic mountain views, and spending time with old friends would do him good. Or maybe he was just trying to escape the crisis. Perhaps this was a cop-out. By the time he arrived at the entrance, his guilt rising, the cop-out side of the argument was winning the day.

As the doors of the lodge opened, Ethan was distracted from his gloomy thoughts by an aroma of freshly baked bread wafting out of the lobby. *That's unusual*, he thought. Most resorts smell like bland, floral chemicals. Inside, he spotted a large sign with three words carved into its surface: TRUST IS EVERYTHING.

Ethan felt his irritation return. If trust was everything, why had no one on the management team told him what was really going on at 10K? But he didn't have time to brood, since a lanky teenager with a cheerful expression was walking toward him.

"Ethan Parker? Welcome to The Grove! I'm Milo. I'll be taking you up to your room."

Ethan blinked. He hadn't realized this would be the kind of place to memorize its guests before they arrived. He knew that happened at some high-end, luxury resorts, but he hadn't expected that sort of treatment at an unassuming place like this. He followed Milo up some stairs that opened out onto an expansive room. He stopped short at the sight of an Aspen tree growing inside the resort's main room.

Milo laughed when he noticed Ethan's amazed expression. "You'll see a few more. The whole place was actually built around a grove of them."

Ethan closed his mouth, realizing it had been hanging open. "Thus the name?" he asked.

"Exactly," said Milo. Apparently the original resort had been really small, with the buildings scattered around some very old Aspens. "When they built the current lodge," he explained, "the trees were so old and beautiful, they didn't feel right cutting them down."

Following Milo through the Great Room and toward the designated suite, Ethan gazed at the open spaces. He liked the thought of designing a lodge around a family of trees!

"Here we are," Milo announced, opening the door to the suite and handing Ethan the key. After Milo showed him around, Ethan dropped into a couch, hoping he hadn't just made a huge mistake.

Pete was the second member of the Brain Trust to arrive, boundless energy and jovial sense of humor intact even after the long flight from Boston. Next came J.J., who had the unique ability to be direct and empathetic at the same time. Everyone saved the big leather couch for Tripper's 6 feet 4 inches. With straight black hair and a laid-back vibe, he was the last to arrive.

As they caught up on each other's lives, Ethan hung back. Pete had convinced him that they could work together on 10K's problems, but as he listened to the good-natured banter, Ethan felt less and less like bringing it up. He knew he could count on this group for advice, but he didn't want to kick the weekend off with such a huge downer.

The truth was, these guys were more than ski buddies, and these weekend getaways more than pure recreation. The annual ski trips had started when the four were in college together. Even as they moved to different cities around the world, they always made time to meet up once a year. The name they had given their band in college, The Brain Trust, had proved especially appropriate especially after all four friends became entrepreneurs. Each had offered the others encouragement, brotherly support, and a kind of personal and professional sounding board that they'd all come to treasure. The four members of the Brain Trust truly *knew* each other and had a unique ability to hold each other accountable, in their businesses as well as in their personal lives.

Listening to the others joking around, Ethan wished he could share what was on his mind. But he just couldn't yet. Luckily, Pete came to his rescue. Reading Ethan's mind, just like Maya had, Pete said, "Let's talk Gazillion Solutions." This was how his friends affectionately referred to 10K.

"Oh . . . you know," Ethan said slowly. "Stressful. Deadlines. Managers to manage. The sweet growth pangs of success. Lonely at the top, boys, lonely at the top." The words sounded hollow even to Ethan. Something his first mentor used to say echoed in his head: "If you are doing leadership alone, you are doing it wrong."

Ethan's transparent attempt to deflect the conversation fooled no one. A brief silence fell over the room. Pete glanced at J.J, then back at Ethan. "All right, here's the deal," Pete clarified. "Gazillion Solutions has hit a roadblock, and I suggested that we spend some time this weekend helping Ethan figure it out."

"Of course," said J.J. sitting forward in his chair. "What's going on? We know you're pretty close to a big delivery date." Tripper propped himself up on an elbow, immediately tuning in to the conversation. Ethan felt a huge weight come off his shoulders and felt a little silly for his earlier hesitation. Tripper, J.J., and Pete would always have his back. And he knew if any one of them were in the same situation, he would want to help.

So Ethan told them all about the May deadline and some sketchy benchmarks in August and November. As he recounted the catastrophic managers' meeting that very morning, Ethan had to admit that he hadn't followed up as closely as he should have. "The crazy thing is, I know we were on track six months ago, and I *think* we were on track three months ago! We've got the chops to pull this thing together and make it hum, but somewhere, somehow, we've gotten lost. It's like that story, you know, about the plane that takes off from New York just half a degree off course, and for the first few hundred miles, no one notices . . ."

"Until they land in Sydney instead of Tokyo," finished Pete.

"Exactly," said Ethan. "But I can't identify that half-degree. Where did we get so off course? And if my executive team had such serious concerns, why am I just learning about them now?"

Tripper spoke up from the couch. "Sounds like you got yourself a trust problem, Park."

"Says the guy who still hasn't settled down?" Ethan shot back before immediately feeling horrible. "I'm sorry man, that was a low blow. I'm pretty shaken up."

Tripper grinned at him, easygoing as always. Tripper had an incredible ability to not take things personally. "No sweat, dude. I've been there—we all have. You've poured everything you have into 10K. Makes sense that you're on edge." Tripper, as unlikely as it seemed, had been the first to strike out on his own, founding his company at twenty-five. He had faced countless setbacks and challenges and had mastered the art of "learn as you go."

"I hadn't really thought much about trust until today," Ethan admitted, voicing the thought that had been nagging at him all afternoon. "But I do trust my team. I don't micromanage, I know they're the experts." But he couldn't deny that something was wrong if they'd all known about the problems and hadn't told him. "At first I thought it was a communication issue, but now I'm thinking it might be accountability. I don't know how things could have gotten this bad if everyone was being held accountable."

"Look," said J.J. "Your team is great. They all seem committed, or you wouldn't have gotten this far. Whatever is going on, there will be a way to course correct." It was a hopeful thought.

"Trust is a fragile thing," added Tripper. "Remember how long it took you to trust me with your guitar in college? You wouldn't let me touch it for years!"

Ethan laughed at the memory. He had saved every penny he earned from his high school job for that instrument, and he treated it like it was made of glass. "Good times man, good times," he said. It felt good to be with friends who knew him better than anyone. And maybe they were right. 10K had some big problems, but maybe they were not as insurmountable as he feared.

"Well I, for one, am exhausted," said Pete. "And we want to get on the mountain as early as possible tomorrow, so I say we call it. We'll dive into this tomorrow at dinner."

Everyone agreed, beat from the long day of travel. Pete clapped his hands together with anticipation: "So who's going to start on the black diamonds with me, eh?"

Ethan smiled broadly for the first time since the disastrous meeting that morning. No matter what happened, he knew he could trust these guys with absolutely anything.

5
COLLISION

ALMOST AT THE CRACK OF DAWN, over a breakfast of perfectly scrambled eggs and piping-hot delicious coffee, the four friends debated the merits of starting slow versus "throwing themselves at the bear," as Pete put it. J.J. voted to spend a few hours on the blue runs to shake out the cobwebs. Ethan agreed. Tripper offered no opinion, so it was counted as two against one. Pete was eventually talked into the warm-up runs, and the group set off.

On the gondola ride up the mountain, Ethan caught a glimpse of Milo taking one of the first runs of the day, one of the perks of working at a ski lodge. He looked like a seasoned pro, well-tucked, skis together, fast but totally in control. Ethan couldn't wait for his first run. These ski trips had been his idea, especially after graduating from college. The friends had scattered, and Ethan wanted to make sure they never lost the connection they'd built. Most years he had arranged the logistics, looking for places three graduate students and a fledgling entrepreneur could afford.

Up top, Ethan sent off a quick picture of the stunning mountain view to Maya. Tripper was the first to push off, and then Ethan hit it hard. "See you guys at the bottom," he shouted.

"Not if we see you first!" J.J. shot back.

Ethan flew down the trail like a comet. There was nothing like that first morning run, and the corduroy was perfect. The snow sliding beneath his skis, the shock of the cold, dry air. He felt the rush of adrenalin that only came from flying down a mountain at high speed. He felt his ski legs come back, and by the middle of the run, he was carving smoothly into each turn.

"Always comes right back!" Ethan said to Tripper, as he coasted to the bottom. "It's great to be back on a mountain again!"

The two skated over to the line for the gondola, ready to head straight back up. They waved to Pete and J.J., who had just reached the bottom.

"I don't think these trips would have happened without you," said Tripper, after the gondola had picked them up. "There were a few years there where it was a real stretch for all four of us. But you always knew exactly how to make it happen. You were relentless!" Amusement tugged at the corner of Tripper's mouth, as he remembered some of the more creative ways Ethan had found to get them together year after year.

Ethan laughed. "Yeah, borrowing that decrepit van to get us from the cheap hostel to the slopes probably wasn't the best plan. Thank goodness Pete knew how to push-start an engine! But hey, we're still here!" *For now*, he thought. If 10K didn't pull out of their nosedive, Ethan might very well end up back in that rusted-out old van. Tripper had a point though, Ethan had never really thought about all the years and all the work that had gone into building his relationships with the Brain Trust.

With one good run behind him, Ethan thought about the situation at 10K with more clarity. Compared to the years of finding a way to get his friends together no matter the challenge, his actions as a leader at 10K now suddenly seemed lackluster. He certainly wasn't a bad boss, and in many ways he thought he was a pretty good one. But he couldn't deny that he'd never put the same level of effort into his relationships with his team.

"You know what, Trip? I think you're right. About the trust issue, I mean."

"Yeah?" Tripper said.

"That guitar—it was true," Ethan explained. "It took me *years* to trust you all. It wasn't because I thought you were irresponsible people, but I had to see how you all handled instruments. I had to see for myself that you all took care of the gear as well as I took care of my guitar." He remembered how good it felt, that his friends knew how much that thing meant to him. No one gave him a hard time about it, or at least, not much of one.

"So what's going on at 10K?" Tripper asked, preparing to hop off the lift as it slowed its approach. "What's the difference?"

"It's embarrassing to admit this, but I don't think I've actually done all that much to earn their trust." They skiers had reached the top of the mountain and the lift deposited them on the packed snow. The distraction gave Ethan the chance to process the thought. When they reached the staging area, he looked ruefully at his friend. "I feel like the world's biggest jerk," he said.

Tripper laughed. "I think most people feel that way sooner or later. Leaders especially—it can be easy to lose sight of reality sometimes. Like I said, trust can be tricky. You have to be really proactive about it. It wasn't enough that we told you we'd be careful with that guitar—you had to see it, and see it over and over again."

Ethan felt like someone had taken a blindfold from his eyes. He couldn't believe he had missed something that fundamental. Maybe instead of a communications issue or an accountability issue, what 10K really had was a leadership issue. It was an unpleasant thought.

J.J. and Pete were just coming off the lift and glided over, smiles huge and faces flushed. "Man, it feels good to get back into this!" Pete said. "What next? Who's hitting that black diamond with me?"

"You know what? I'm in!" said Ethan. The last thing he wanted to be thinking about up on this mountain was the idea that 10K's problems were a personal failure on his part. He wanted to rush down the mountain again, cold air and speed distracting him from a problem he wasn't sure he felt equipped to handle. He looked out at the white-flecked pines and aspens flanking the treacherous ski trail Pete had indicated, its blanket of fresh snow concealing dozens of moguls. It looked vicious and delicious, and Ethan wanted to show it who was boss. He and Pete made their way over to the black diamond run, while J.J. and Tripper stuck to the blue.

"See you on the other side!" Ethan shouted to Pete, and launched himself down the slope. On the steeper hill, he flew across the snow, carving between the mounds with a vengeance. Just as he felt himself lift off the edge of a mogul, Milo came into view ahead of him, minding his own business, loving the wicked run. Ethan jerked his skis to avoid Milo, but as a result, hooked an edge and sent himself into a hands-free nosedive down the steep slope.

As Ethan landed, a lightning bolt of pain exploded up his left leg. He crumpled in a heap and slid yards down the slope in what felt like slow motion. Rolling to a stop, he heard his own ragged breathing. Pain pulsed upward through his body. He lifted his head a few degrees and saw Milo, who was also huffing and puffing.

Ethan started to struggle up to a sitting position, but Milo shouted, "Stop!" The kid jammed one ski pole into the snow just at the downslope edge of Ethan's lower ski, then stabbed in his other pole, effectively pinning Ethan's ski in place and preventing it from slipping even an inch.

"Stay still!" Milo commanded urgently. Ethan stayed still. He was in a world of pain.

A moment later, another skier swung into view, spraying a thin curtain of snow in the air as he carved to a quick halt. The skier spoke in short, deliberate syllables. Ethan had no idea what he was saying. *I must be in shock,* he thought.

The man put away his phone, looked at Milo and said, "Good work." He then turned to Ethan. "Don't move," he said. "Ski Patrol is on its way." Within minutes, Ethan found himself enjoying a personal sleigh ride down the mountain. Given the mix of searing pain and humiliation, "enjoying" was probably not the most accurate term. An ambulance greeted him and rushed him to the local hospital. The rescue skier never left his side.

"There's good news and bad news," said the doctor as she studied the MRI images on her computer screen. The rural mountain emergency room had not been too crowded. Ethan had been signed in and sent straight into X-ray and then to the MRI department in fairly short order, with just enough time to text Maya and reassure her that he was in no real danger. The doctor carried herself with a relaxed confidence that Ethan found reassuring.

"Good news first, please," he said.

Facing Ethan, she held out a pencil between them, holding it upright like a post. "Think of your tibia, your shinbone, as a pillar. It's one of the largest and strongest bones in your body, because it bears a lot of weight." She touched the pencil's pink eraser. "What you've got is a compression fracture of the tibial plateau. It's kind of a complicated break. You can't cast it; all you can do is ice it, wrap it, elevate it, brace it, and stay off of it."

"Remind me," said Ethan. "This is the good news?"

She smiled. "The good-news part is there's no torn meniscus, no other structural damage, just the fracture. With a fracture like this, we sometimes see fragments of bone break off at the edge of the plateau, and when that happens, you're in danger of that whole side of the plateau collapsing, which would have forced us into surgery, and not the prettiest kind." Apparently the quick action of the rescue personnel on the mountain had saved Ethan's leg from a lot of damage.

"I was completely immobilized," he recalled. "That was Milo who did that." His blurred memory of the accident was already fading, but he clearly remembered Milo's voice and his direct command to Ethan that he not move. "He wouldn't let me move an inch."

She nodded. "He did you a big favor, Mr. Parker."

Ethan took a deep breath, then asked the doctor, "And the bad news?"

"Not really that bad. But this knee is going to take some major TLC. You'll be on crutches for some time, of course. And no flying, not for at least a week; we'll have to see how it goes. You've got some pretty severe swelling here, and until that inflammation comes down, there's still a very real possibility of blood clots. I'll want to keep you here for a few more hours and give it another look in the evening before we release you. And we'll want to get you back in here to look at things, say, this Thursday."

No flying for at least a week? Ethan's mind reeled. His company was in crisis. If there was ever a time when he needed to be in the office full-time, overtime, for days on end, it was now—and he had to stay put in Colorado, hobbling around on crutches at a ski resort . . . for a week?

6
THE READING ROOM

WHEN ETHAN'S CAB PULLED UP to the entrance of The Grove, Milo came out the front doors to greet him. "Here's your new room key, Mr. Parker. 108, on the first floor." It was an accessible room, so moving around would be a little easier to manage with the crutches. The lodge would take care of transferring Ethan's baggage later that evening. "Just let the front desk know when you would like them to pick it up," Milo said.

"Oh," said Ethan, a bit surprised because he hadn't yet told The Grove about his change of plans.

He must have looked confused because Milo explained. "We had an inkling you were going to need a new room when we sent you off to the ER with your knee looking the way it was. Your tab is being picked up by the lodge, including meals and incidentals, for as long as you need to stay. We're no strangers to ski injuries, and we figured you might be needing a few extra days here. It's the least we can do—we're very sorry about your accident."

Ethan thanked Milo and asked who else he could speak to. This level of care and generosity was something he had rarely encountered, and he wanted to make sure he expressed his gratitude.

"That would be Sunny Bonaventure," Milo said with a mischievous grin. "She was so distressed to hear about your accident she almost came down to the hospital. I'm sure she'll be checking in on you." Ethan tried to pay Milo something for his trouble, but he insisted: "All taken care of. And besides, I got to call in sick from school to help out!"

Ethan hadn't taken three hobbling steps into the lobby before his friends crowded around him. They had been waiting in front of the toasty fire in the Great Room.

"There's the pro!" called Pete.

"Dude, this is the worst," said J.J.

Tripper said nothing and put a hand on Ethan's shoulder.

"Yeah, this will teach me to hit the moguls first thing," Ethan said, grimacing.

"Listen," said J.J. "We've talked it over and decided that tomorrow we're all going to stay in. We'll camp out here, sit in front of this awesome fireplace, and help you hammer out what's going on at Gazillion Solutions. Okay?"

"No, you won't," countered Ethan. "You guys are supposed to be out on the slopes. I'd be miserable if I knew the powder was out there and you three weren't in it." The offer was generous, and was exactly what Ethan would have done if it had been one of the others in the splint. "You all came to ski. Plus, as much as I don't want to, I'm going to need to rest."

Pete and J.J. hesitated, wearing the same look of uncertainty. Tripper finally clapped him on the shoulder and said, "All right, but tomorrow night we are going to have that strategy session. No excuses! You look about ready to fall over. Let's call it for tonight." Management had let them know about Ethan's new room, and they'd already ordered room service.

Ethan smiled blearily at his friends. Suddenly the fatigue hit him all at once, on top of the brain fog from his pain meds. "You guys are too much," he said.

The next morning, Ethan was brooding in his room with his leg on a few pillows. His friends had made one more round of protest before he convinced them not to sacrifice their full day on the mountain. He had won by pointing out that spending eight hours talking about his problems wasn't exactly his own idea of fun. Yet here he was, replaying the conference room disaster in his mind. He'd already had a nice long call with Maya. She'd wanted to fly out as soon as she'd heard about the accident, but her doctor had said a flat no to flying this close to term in her pregnancy. Feeling a need to get out of his room, Ethan hobbled out on his crutches, heading toward the common areas of the lodge. About halfway down the hall, he noticed a single elevator with an ornate sign above the metal doors that said: READING ROOM. Intrigued, Ethan decided to investigate.

The elevator only offered a single option as a destination, and when the doors opened, they revealed a large, silent room, with overstuffed leather chairs and long, deep couches. There were polished mahogany end tables and coffee tables and reading lamps everywhere. To the right and left, the walls were lined with massive bookshelves. As in the Great Room, the far wall consisted of huge plateglass windows looking out onto the mountainside.

As Ethan hobbled along one of the walls of books, he noticed a modest-sized portrait of an older man in a recessed niche. It looked like it had been painted in the 1940s, the man's pale face floating in a sea of black. A pair of delicate, gold-rimmed spectacles was tucked into his suit pocket and he wore a kind, friendly expression. The small gold plaque at the base of the frame identified the man as Richard Bonaventure.

"This was Richard's favorite room. He designed it himself." The voice startled Ethan. He looked up and saw a woman closing a discrete door tucked into a corner. She had the weathered complexion of a lifetime skier and a warm smile that reminded him of Milo's affable grin.

"Oh, hello," he said, slowly rotating himself around on the crutches.

"Sunny Bonaventure," she said, walking toward Ethan with her hand outstretched. "I'm glad to have caught you—I wanted to check on you personally after the accident. I'm glad you found your way up here. Richard was interested in anything and everything, so he made the library the heart of the lodge."

So this was the owner of The Grove! Sunny seemed much more relaxed and at ease than he would have expected from a busy executive. When Milo said that the owner wanted to check in on him, he had expected a short, brusque interaction, peppered with the usual customer service jargon and formalities.

"Ethan Parker," he said, reaching out to take the hand she offered. "You have an amazing place here." He nodded toward the portrait. "So you knew Mr. Bonaventure?"

"He was my grandfather," she said.

Ethan felt sheepish. "Of course—the pain meds must be making me a little slow. Anyway, I owe you a big thanks. My room. The week. It's all very generous of you and completely unexpected."

"We like to take care of our guests," Sunny said, "especially if they get hurt on the mountain. We have a habit of covering any stay that is prolonged by a serious injury." Then, to Ethan's surprise, she said, "As it happens, I'm familiar with 10K Solutions. You're doing some really exciting work. I was planning to introduce myself even before you decided to cartwheel your way down the mountain." There was a mischievous twinkle in her eyes.

Ethan liked her sense of humor. "I guess that's an accurate description of what happened," he said with a laugh. "I promise I don't usually take such irresponsible risks on the slopes."

Sunny waved a hand dismissively. "We've seen much worse around here, believe me. The excitement of your first few runs of the season is a feeling we all can relate to."

Ethan felt at ease in Sunny's presence. She was passionate about her sport and her business, two things he also cared deeply about. She had piqued his curiosity, and he asked, "Why would a ski lodge owner know about a scrappy software startup in Minneapolis?"

"Oh, I have a wide range of interests." Turns out, she had worked in the tech world before taking over the family business. "I still follow what's going on in tech," she said.

Ethan glanced at the portrait again, then back at Sunny. "Apple doesn't fall very far from the tree?"

She looked for a moment as if there was a story to tell, then said, "My grandfather built this place from the ground up." Richard Bonaventure had led The Grove to stunning success by the time he retired, she explained, and turned it over to his son, Richard Bonaventure II, whom everyone called Richie. "My father was a good man," Sunny said, "but he nearly drove the lodge into the ground."

"Ouch," said Ethan, looking around the gorgeously appointed library. "So what happened? He must have done something to turn things around."

"Actually," said Sunny, "what happened next was, he died: a sudden heart attack." Her grandfather had considered coming back and taking the reins again, but Sunny knew that would've been too much for him. "So I did the only thing I could to keep it in the family. I quit my job and moved back home to run the lodge myself."

The Grove's history hit a little close to home. *The place had lost its way.* Ethan felt like 10K was losing its way too. "Things seem to be running well now," he said. "What did you do to get it back?"

"Well. . . ," she said, her voice trailing off as she sat back into a deep chair. "By that time, I'd seen it all in the corporate world—the good, the bad, and yes, the ugly. I saw a lot wrong with the way things were being run, which only reinforced a slogan I learned from my grandfather: Trust is the central currency of business."

Trust again. His conversation with Tripper suddenly came back to him. "You make it sound simple," Ethan said, "but I'm sure it wasn't." Trust seemed like the theme of the weekend. On a whim, he said, "You know, I have an enormous problem waiting for me at 10K. Would you be willing to share any thoughts or advice for someone in a similar position?"

"I'd love to," Sunny said brightly. "But first you must be hungry. Why don't I go down and order some lunch, then we can talk?"

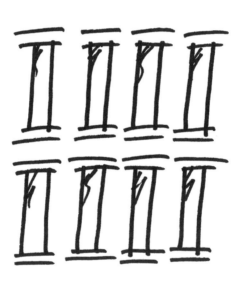

7
THE 8 PILLARS

WHILE SUNNY WAS GONE, Ethan resumed his slow, awkward circuit around the Reading Room. Through the expansive window, he could see skiers in the distance, tiny action figures zigzagging their way down the slope. Ethan felt a pang of jealousy and frowned at his swollen knee, still aching and sensitive. Any misstep with the crutches resulted in a flash of pain that reminded him why he was here in this room and not carving down the slopes. *Serves me right,* he thought. *I have no business being on this vacation in the first place. What kind of leader leaves for a ski vacation in the middle of a crisis?* He crutched back over to the chair and sat down again. All the worry and guilt he had managed to suppress crept back into his thoughts.

A gentle chime announced the arrival of the elevator, saving Ethan from his downward spiral, and Sunny stepped into the room carrying two covered plates that smelled delicious.

"Enjoying the view?" Sunny asked, placing the plates on a small table next to Ethan's chair. "There is something so calming about watching the mountain from this room. It's like a snow globe come to life."

Ethan smiled. She was right—the floor-to-ceiling windows made him feel like he was looking out into the world's biggest snow globe. "Honestly I feel pretty guilty," he said. "Things at 10K are not going well, and I only found out the morning I left for this trip. I should have stayed home."

Sunny gave him a sympathetic look. "Well, I would love to help in any way I can. Turning The Grove around wasn't easy, and there were plenty of moments where I thought we were done for." Even with all of the years in industry behind her, and her lifelong relationships with many of the staff, there were days when Sunny wanted to give up and sell the place to the highest bidder. "But we stuck with it, and I consider running The Grove to be my proudest accomplishment."

There was something about her willingness to share her challenges so freely that gave Ethan the courage to open up. "This may sound weird, okay?" he started. "But I've got a problem, at my company. More like four problems, really. I think we have a major communication problem, a leadership problem, an accountability issue. And on top of it all, I think I might have a trust issue somewhere but I have no idea where it came from."

Sunny listened thoughtfully, then nodded. "I understand the question and the dilemma you are facing." She thought for another moment, then said, "I can't speak to the specifics of your situation. But I can tell you this: In my experience, a communication problem is never a communication problem. Not at its root. It's a symptom of the actual problem."

Ethan's heart sank. "So it's really a leadership problem."

"Actually, no," said Sunny. "Another symptom."

Ethan blinked a few times. "And accountability? Don't tell me. Another symptom?"

Sunny shrugged. "Well . . . probably, yes."

He put his face in his hands. This was not encouraging. "Okay, I give up—symptoms of what?"

"Can I ask you a sort of personal question?" she asked. Ethan spread his hands out as if to say, of course. "What you're sharing about the situation with your business . . . Why are you sharing this with *me*?"

He almost regretted his openness, but although he had only just met Sunny Bonaventure, he already felt completely at ease in her presence. "Because I thought you might have some advice."

Sunny nodded. "Okay, I get that. But why?"

Ethan shrugged. "I guess because I feel like I can trust you. I mean, I hardly know you, but, yeah, I feel like I can trust you."

There was an amused twinkle in her eyes. "Even though we've only just met?" Ethan wasn't sure what to say, so he didn't say anything. "Trust is much more complex than most people realize," Sunny continued. "We've made something of a study of it here. It was really our discoveries about trust that made The Grove what it is today. My big revelation was when I realized that nothing is really a leadership problem, or a communication problem, or even a customer service problem. At the core, everything is really a trust problem."

"Like the sign in the lobby," said Ethan, remembering its prominent placement. "Trust is everything."

"Exactly!" she said. "Once we realized this, we were able to address everything that had gone wrong. Nothing will sink a business faster than a breakdown in trust."

Ethan really wanted to know how The Grove had lost its way. "Was there some big betrayal? How did things go from good to bad?" Maybe hearing about what went wrong could help him figure out what might have caused the problems at his own company.

"Oh nothing like that!" said Sunny. "Trust isn't that straightforward. My father was a wonderful man, and he cared deeply about the lodge and his employees. He would never have knowingly done anything harmful. The issues were much deeper."

According to Sunny, when her father was younger, he went to

business school and came back with all sorts of exciting concepts, which he proceeded to apply to The Grove. "Well, he went a little overboard," she continued, "and ended up trying out every new thing he'd heard about. He'd change the structures and the metrics and the expectations constantly. He always thought he was making the best choices for the business, but the result was that the employees never knew where they stood." After years and years of this, Sunny explained, trust had eroded so badly that there was barely any left. "He was a trustworthy man, but he had not built a trustworthy business."

Ethan felt a twinge of frustration. Nothing Sunny said felt terribly relevant to his predicament. He'd never been dishonest with his employees, and he didn't change things up on them the way Richie had. How could he have built an untrustworthy business? Ethan wasn't even sure what that meant. "I don't think I completely understand," he said. "How can a business be untrustworthy? Did they lie to patrons? Were people embezzling?"

Suddenly embarrassed, he realized he had probably just inadvertently insulted Sunny's father, and he barely knew the woman! "I'm so sorry—I didn't mean to imply . . . " he trailed off, his cheeks bright red.

Sunny smiled reassuringly and waved away his fears. "No need to apologize. It's a natural misunderstanding. Trust is more than the big things. It can fade slowly over time. There isn't always a major breach of honesty. That was what happened here." The trust problems started showing up in all sorts of ways, she explained. Sometimes it masqueraded as a leadership problem, sometimes as a customer service problem, sometimes as departmental divisions, but at the root of it all was trust.

Ethan thought about his own management team. "Well, we definitely have departmental siloing going on," he said. "That was what made me think we have a communication problem. And I realized yesterday that I probably haven't been doing a good enough job to build my team's trust in me. But I don't really know how to go about doing that." It seemed like such a huge problem—he didn't know where to start.

"Ahh," said Sunny sympathetically. "I think I can help you with that. After years of reflecting on what made The Grove work so well, we identified eight areas that seem to drastically increase trust in a person or an organization. When you focus on improving these skills and practicing them all the time, you can begin to build and rebuild trust organically." She grabbed a napkin from the catering tray and a pen from her pocket. She quickly sketched out a picture and handed it to Ethan.

Ethan gazed at the napkin. It looked like a Greek temple with eight columns.

"We call them the 8 Pillars of Trust—consistency, clarity, compassion, character, contribution, competency, connection, and commitment," Sunny said. "They're like guideposts. When everyone focuses on excelling in these eight dimensions, organizations begin to thrive and grow. Trust increases, and so does everything else."

"I guess this makes sense," Ethan responded, a bit hesitant. He supposed some of these things had to do with trust. Consistency made sense. He could see how being unreliable would lead someone to lose trust in you. But some of the others pillars just seemed like they came out of left field.

"They can be a little hard to visualize at first," Sunny said, anticipating his reaction. "How about this—since you're going to be our guest for the next week, why don't I introduce you to some of our staff? They can show you around and you can see our philosophies in action. It can be difficult to explain in the abstract."

Well, thought Ethan. *What else am I going to do?* "That's a kind offer, Sunny, thank you. I need all the help I can get."

"Wonderful. I'll set some things up and be in touch tomorrow. In the meantime, please feel free to make use of any and all of the facilities. And never hesitate to reach out to anyone."

Ethan shook the hand she offered then sank into the leather chair, looking out over the snowy vista. Perhaps this week wouldn't be a complete loss after all.

CONNECTION

8
A STRONG FOUNDATION

THE LIGHT WAS JUST STARTING TO FADE when the other members of the Brain Trust returned from the slopes, cheeks pink with sunburn, the imprint of their ski goggles vivid on their faces. Ethan was waiting for them in the Great Room, reading *Prince Caspian*, which he had borrowed from the Reading Room in a fit of nostalgia. J.J. spotted him and waved enthusiastically as the group headed over. They seemed tired and happy after what had looked to Ethan like a perfect day to be out on the mountain.

Tripper flung himself down on the couch next to Ethan. "Dude, we definitely need to put this place into the rotation. The slopes are fantastic!" He sighed and stretched out, settling into the cushions. "We've got to come back next year, bare minimum. You are going to love some of the runs. And the views are epic."

Ethan mimed a knife to his heart "You're killing me!" he said, mostly joking. Mostly. "I'm glad you guys had a good time. It looked like a great day to be out."

"Yes, but the most important question now," said Pete with mock seriousness, "is après-ski! What delicious things are on order?"

Ethan beamed. After his meeting with Sunny in the Reading Room, he had hobbled down to the restaurant to ask about dinner reservations. He was referred to a woman named Naomi, the director of community. Like the rest of the staff at The Grove, she already knew who Ethan was and had heard all about his accident. When he requested a dinner reservation, she had given him a conspiratorial glance and said, "I think I can do you one better."

"I managed to arrange something special, actually," he said to the Brain Trust. "The lodge is putting a menu together and bringing it to us, right here!" Naomi had pointed out that maneuvering in and out of the restaurant would be inconvenient on crutches, and their small suite was just not suited to dinner for four. Instead, she had proposed they dine right up against the window overlooking the mountains, next to one of the three enormous fireplaces.

"Perfect," said J.J. "Dinner without even having to move? Nothing could be better. I am absolutely wrecked."

At that very moment, Milo and another staff member rolled in a catering cart that was overflowing with steaming plates, bowls, and platters. "Hello Mr. Parker!" Milo said, with his usual cheer. "How's your knee?"

"Oh, it's hanging in there," Ethan replied. "Milo, these are my friends—J.J., Pete, and Tripper." Each man nodded in turn. "Milo is the reason my knee wasn't completely destroyed. The doctor told me that the way he pinned my skis probably saved me from needing surgery."

Milo flushed from the praise as he and his colleague set about putting plates and serving dishes out on the low table in front of the couches. "We hope you like what we've put together for you. Lou pulled out all the stops!" Milo grinned at his colleague, who was just arranging the last platter. The man was not dressed all in black like the waiters Ethan had seen earlier in the restaurant. He noticed the man was wearing a white coat and checkered black-and-white pants—a personal visit from the chef!

"Ethan, I'd like to present Chef Lou, The Grove's chef de cuisine."

In a booming voice, Lou said, "That we did, Milo, The Grove's famous lasagna. Nothing beats it after a day on the slopes!"

Ethan looked up at the big man, surprised and flattered. Pete beat him to a response: "You have my unending gratitude sir!" Gesturing at the feast now covering the low table, Pete said, "This looks absolutely fit for royalty."

It was true—the serving plates were presented family style, with piles of vegetables and two different salads, but in front of each member of the Brain Trust was an individual steaming crock of the most glorious lasagna Ethan had ever seen. It was a perfect après-ski dinner, even if he had missed the "ski" part.

"You are more than welcome!" said Chef Lou, "and I have a special desert planned for you too. I'll be back with that when you're ready!" He and Milo bustled away with the carts, leaving the four to their meal.

"Wow," said J.J., looking over the expansive spread with appreciation. "This is spectacular! How did you swing something like this?"

"I have to tell you," said Ethan, as he plunged his fork into the layers of pasta, cheese, and red sauce. "I've never been to a ski lodge quite like this one. Everyone I've met is going above and beyond in just about every way possible. I even met the owner, Sunny Bonaventure, today—she talked me through some of my issues with 10K."

"Ah yes. Gazillion Solutions! No more avoiding the topic, my friend," said Pete. "The time has come."

Ethan sighed. "I don't even know anymore, man. Sunny was telling me about some of the methodology they use here. It all sounds great, but I don't really see how it's going to solve 10K's problems. This idea that I have a trust problem keeps coming up, but I don't know what went wrong. If I don't know what I did to lose my employees' trust, how can I go about fixing it?"

J.J. had some ideas. "Okay, let's see if we can come at this another way. Clearly some folks on your team haven't felt like they can tell you how behind things are, right? So what are your relationships with them like? What are their biggest challenges? How engaged are they?"

Fair questions, Ethan thought, sitting back from his plate. "I mean, I think good? I've always thought of myself as a different kind of leader. I trust my people to be the experts in their field, and I try not to meddle." He prided himself on hanging back, looking at the big picture, and letting them manage their own divisions. "I hated being micromanaged, and I promised myself when I started 10K that no one who worked there would ever feel like their initiative was being quashed."

"That's a great philosophy," Tripper chimed in, wiping a bit of sauce off his chin, "but I think J.J. was getting at something different. Even though you don't tell them all what to do, you still must have some level of connection or rapport with them—what about that? I find most issues can be solved as long as I have a strong existing relationship."

Ethan was silent, as a distinct wave of discomfort washed over him. In the early days, 10K Solutions had been a well-oiled machine. Everyone worked together so easily it felt automatic. People had been younger, so they often stayed late or socialized outside of work hours. In recent years, though, he hadn't spent nearly as much time with the growing staff of the company. In fact, he barely had time to meet with anyone on a regular basis.

"Well, I mean, we have good working relationships." Ethan realized how flimsy this sounded.

"You know, we had an issue recently that sounds similar to yours," said J.J. "Last year I realized we had so much interdepartmental conflict I had to bring in a third party to help." At well over four hundred employees, J.J's company had scaled faster than any of the other companies founded by the Brain Trust. Ethan couldn't imagine facing a breakdown like that with a company almost three times the size of 10K.

J.J. recounted that dodgy period, explaining how he'd brought in a third-party consultant. "Instead of doing a fact-finding process or a structural reorganization, they had every single employee do a self-reflection exercise. I can't remember each step right now, but it was a graphic that looked like a shield, like a personal coat of arms." The exercise asked employees to identify things like values, personal passions, strengths, areas for improvement, and so on. "Everyone had to fill this out, and then the consultant put together smaller groups to talk about what they had written. They even rotated so everyone shared with at least a few small groups. It was pretty straightforward, but the results were transformational."

Pete, ever skeptical, was giving J.J. a side-eye as he helped himself to another scoop of vegetables. "What happened?"

Ethan shared Pete's skepticism. It sounded more like a summer camp icebreaker than a strategy for a software company.

J.J. shrugged. "I know it sounds a little cheesy, or even contrived, but I couldn't argue with the results. Even people who'd worked together for years said they learned more about each other in a few minutes than in all their years as colleagues." As J.J. figured, there were two major benefits: The first was that everyone who did the exercise had the chance to reflect on their own answers. "It actually helped me to understand myself better, and I think it's made me a better leader."

"And the second?" Pete asked, looking more thoughtfully at J.J. now. When J.J. took something seriously it was almost always worth paying attention.

"The second wasn't what I expected, actually," J.J. said, lowering his voice. "When everyone shared, there were as many or more differences between folks than similarities. But even the differences seemed to bring people together. I don't think it was really about finding out what we had in common. It made the folks I work with more human. Suddenly I wasn't working with 'that woman in Operations.' I was working with Jane, who has three kids, values humor, and who has an award-winning collection of rare orchids."

Ethan marveled at how tuned in the Brain Trust was. He thought he knew his team pretty well, but not this well. Years ago, when the Brain Trust made music together, each person knew what the other was doing even before they did it. Each person knew what the other was *thinking* before they said it! Here they were, twenty some years later, and J.J. got straight to the heart of a problem at 10K without even having been there.

10K had been like that at first—Ethan had almost forgotten that. But of course, they grew fast. Today the company couldn't even fit a full leadership team meeting in his living room. He didn't know the names of all the employees anymore, let alone their spouses or kids. This conversation was making him realize how much he wanted to get that feeling back.

"That sounds really great, J.J., really," said Ethan. "But I don't know how it would help us with a deadline just a few months away, you know?"

"You might be surprised," responded J.J., grabbing a bread roll to soak up the rich red sauce. "We noticed a difference right away. Teams started working more effectively together. A few deadlines we almost missed came through. You should give it a shot."

Ethan thought about this for a few moments, enjoying the last of his lasagna. "I can see how that would help people connect with each other. And if we felt more connected as a leadership team, it probably wouldn't have taken so long for someone to speak up about the delays and the problems." Ethan thought about the 8 Pillar sketch that Sunny had drawn for him that morning, which now served as a bookmark in *Prince Caspian*. **CONNECTION** was one of the pillars, and hearing the story about J.J.'s shield exercise was helping him see how it might increase trust.

Before Ethan had a chance to ask J.J. for more details, Chef

Lou arrived, wheeling in another cart, shrouded in white table-cloths. Naomi, who had arranged their little feast, was with him.

"I hope you all are ready for dessert!" boomed the chef, looking approvingly at the empty plates and serving platters. "And may I introduce Naomi Brewer, our director of community. This event was all her idea."

The four expressed their appreciation, complimented Chef Lou on the food, and thanked Naomi for arranging such a perfect dining spot. Lou had been busy while they talked, and suddenly Ethan looked down at the dessert in front of him. It was a bowl of homemade vanilla ice cream, flecked with real vanilla beans, and gingersnap cookies, still warm from the oven.

Ethan looked up at Naomi in surprise. "How did you . . . ," he trailed off. This was his favorite desert. When he was a boy, Ethan and his dad would go out in the winter to the lake, cut some ice, bring it home, and use it for freezing truly homemade ice cream. Pure vanilla, sugar, raw eggs, and fresh cream from the dairy farm next door were the only ingredients. Cranked by hand, the ice cream tasted like heaven, and nothing—not even those high-class brands that called themselves "homemade" or "old-fashioned"—came remotely close.

"I'm so glad you like it!" said Naomi, delighted that the surprise had made such an impact. "It's part of our culture here—we're always looking for ways to surprise people with special treatment. It's part of The Grove experience."

Ethan took a bite of the ice cream and cookies. It was every bit as good as it looked. "But how did you know?" he asked. His friends were already digging in, looking at each other with smug expressions.

"Oh, a little birdie told us," Naomi said, glancing at Ethan's friends. "Sunny mentioned to me that she's been telling you about our trust framework—this is one of the ways that we foster the compassion pillar. We want guests of the mountain to feel truly valued and appreciated."

"But I mean," said Ethan, still not quite believing that The Grove kitchen had gone to all this trouble. "This is so specific!"

Shaking her head, Naomi said, "This one wasn't even that hard to pull off. I already happened to know that Lou here loves making our ice cream in house."

Ethan thought about what Sunny had said earlier about the special kind of culture at The Grove. He was experiencing it now. "This all was very generous of you."

"You're very welcome," said Chef Lou, as he departed the Great Room, leaving the friends to enjoy their dessert. "And there's plenty where that came from! Just ask anyone at the restaurant when you are ready for more. Should be enough ice cream and cookies to last you the whole week."

It was music to Ethan's ears (and his stomach).

9
THE TREEHOUSE VIEW

ON SUNDAY MORNING Ethan woke up with the guys, who were planning to get a few early runs in before they all had to head home. Feeling inspired by the previous night's conversations over their meal in the Great Room, Ethan wanted to dive right into action. He wanted to try out J.J.'s shield exercise, but it sounded like something better done when the Brain Trust could all be together in person. He could at least set up some one-on-one video calls for the coming week, though. Considering connection and the conversation with Naomi and Lou, Ethan wanted to at least try to maintain some of that while he was stuck in Colorado. He was also thinking about his team back at 10K—it was time let them know he'd be stuck in Colorado for a while.

Maneuvering slowly on his crutches, Ethan made his way to the Great Room and ordered coffee, before settling in one of the leather chairs in front of the roaring fire. Opening his laptop, he began drafting emails to 10K's division heads, Iris, Dom, Zach, and Jenna. Just then a young man Ethan had seen at the front desk approached him.

"Excuse me, Mr. Parker?" he asked, introducing himself as Nick. "Sunny wanted me to let you know that our leadership meeting is this afternoon. She said you might be interested in attending." Ethan must have looked confused. Nick explained that The Grove held their leadership meetings on weekends, which was peak time for the lodge and everyone was usually working. He held out a folded card on the resort's branded stationary.

Taking the card, Ethan thanked Nick and read the note:

Ethan—

I'd love to have you attend our weekly leadership meeting this afternoon. It will be a great way to see some of our methodology in action. 3:00. Meet me in the Reading Room.

—Sunny

Ethan didn't love the sound of sitting through a long meeting, but he didn't want to be rude. And he trusted that Sunny wouldn't suggest it if she didn't think it would help him. He let Nick know that he would be happy to attend.

Ethan spent the morning writing emails explaining about his accident and that he was going to be stuck in Colorado for at least a week. He requested a leadership meeting for first thing Monday morning and one-on-one meetings with everyone. He made an extra effort to be friendly in his messages; his usual emails were short and to the point, but now he wondered if that tone might be contributing to a feeling of disconnection. He thought about the first boss he ever had, a man named Milton Foster, who had asked about Ethan's family on a regular basis. It had never felt forced or false, and it was clear that Milton genuinely cared about everyone who worked for him. Ethan felt a little ashamed he had lost that habit. He'd always wanted to live up to the example Milton had set.

A few hours later, Ethan's friends came down the mountain. Unfortunately they needed to pack their gear and head home. The

Brain Trust gathered in the Great Room to say their goodbyes, already planning next year's getaway.

"Good luck with everything, man," said Pete, thrusting his hand out for a firm shake from Ethan. "We believe in you. And we are here for you any way we can help."

"Seriously, Park," said J.J. "When you're back home again, let's set up a conference call, and keep talking this thing through, okay?"

Tripper leaned in and gave Ethan's shoulder a squeeze. "You got this, man."

At 2:50, Ethan made his way up to the Reading Room to meet Sunny. She led him to a back corner, where they entered a separate elevator that was so well hidden behind a bookshelf, it felt like a secret passage. The elevator brought them up one additional level, where the doors opened to a very small, octagonal room with a truly spectacular 360-degree view of the mountain.

"Welcome to the Treehouse!" said Sunny.

"Wow," said Ethan, scanning the majesty before him. "I thought the Reading Room had the best view in the place, but this tops it!"

"Literally," said Sunny, clearly pleased to share the beautiful space.

There were already eight people gathered around the table, chatting with relaxed familiarity. It was a world of difference from the tense silence of Ethan's own leadership team meeting of just a few days ago. Once everyone was settled, Sunny welcomed the group and gave Ethan an official introduction, with a brief rundown of 10K's history. Ethan was startled at just how much she knew about his little company and its contributions to the industry.

Chef Lou was there, and Sunny turned to him to kick off the meeting. "How's Jamie doing?" she asked.

"Doin' good, doin' good." The chef's voice filled the octagonal room. Ethan had not picked up on it last night, but Lou was definitely a New Yorker. "Got him in a nice little place of his own, a box, basically, but it's clean, and it's in a good neighborhood."

"And he's good?" she asked.

"Clean and sober, going on six months this week!" said Chef Lou. This brought a slew of supportive comments from everyone. "Way to go! Nice, Lou."

Sunny turned to the woman seated next to Chef Lou, and said, "Amirah? Where are we on the new inventory system?" She was The Grove's director of finance.

"I've got it narrowed down to two vendors," Amirah said, and sketched out the features of two competing software products. Each system employed A.I. to project the lodge's supply needs over time and used data from weather forecasting, economic news, and other inputs to predict the ebb and flow of occupancy rates. Ethan loved the concept.

"We want to do a test run of both systems for the next sixty days," she explained, "to see if there's one we really like."

Sunny nodded, then said, "How?"

"We set up two dedicated laptops, one for each system," Amirah continued, "and will run them both completely independently so we get untainted results."

Focusing intently, Sunny repeated, "How?"

It reminded Ethan of Pete's young son, and how he'd gone through a phase where every other sentence started out with "Why?" Only in this case the repeated question was "How?"

As if she expected Sunny's questions, Amirah was ready: "I hired a sharp college kid, Jerome. He'll feed our data in remotely, twice a day, and come in once a week to do printouts and collate results into a weekly summary for us. He starts Wednesday.

Sunny nodded once and responded simply: "Fantastic." And she moved on to the person sitting next to Amirah, whom Ethan now recognized as the one who, two days earlier, had driven his rescue toboggan ride. "Bob?" prompted Sunny.

And it went on like that, with Sunny inquiring about a single project, asking where they were with it, prompting them with the question "How?" She nodded when she seemed satisfied with the level of clarity, ready to move on to the next topic.

That was it. No detailed progress reports. No lengthy agenda. It was clear that everyone came prepared for this style of meeting. Ethan couldn't help but compare this gathering to the meeting he'd conducted on Thursday morning. The feeling was so different here; it was personable and warm, yet efficient. And the whole thing was over in a mere twenty minutes, with no ambiguity about next steps.

Ethan wished his own meetings could be more like this one. Everyone shared a final "how" on which they would take action, in most cases by the next day. And there were the 8 Pillars again, Ethan realized. Everything in that meeting had been clearly stated, direct, and to the point. He remembered Sunny's sketch and realized he must be watching the pillar of **CLARITY** in action.

At the end of the meeting, Sunny brought up the mission statement, which she had displayed on the wall in the tiny octagonal Treehouse:

> *Because life is hectic, we give every member of our community a fulfilling mountain experience.*

Ethan had already seen this statement a few times—in a brochure in the Great Room, on an oak plank in his guest room, even at the bottom of the menu in the dining room. He hadn't given it much thought, but evidently they had. The conversation went on for another ten minutes, and everyone shared an example of something they'd done or planned to do that was connected to the mission.

After the others had left, Ethan turned to Sunny. "That mission statement, is that new?"

"Actually, we've had it for twelve years," Sunny said. "But we make sure to talk through it at least once a month."

Ethan wondered about that. "Don't they know all this already?"

She thought for a moment about the question, before responding with one of her own. "Can I ask you a personal question? You're married, right?"

Ethan beamed. "Eight years now with a baby due soon!"

"Do you ever tell your wife you love her?" Sunny asked.

"Every day," he said.

"Why? I mean, doesn't she already know all that already?"

Now it clicked—he understood.

"Most mission statements get put into logos and email signatures," Sunny explained, "maybe even painted on a wall somewhere, and are promptly forgotten. But the mission statement is truly our guiding philosophy. A mission statement should inspire action every day. When people really internalize the mission, the way they make decisions and the way they do their jobs is different. They act in a way that is more aligned with who we want to be as an organization." She gazed out the window at the expansive view. Ethan could see not only The Grove's own mountain but a breathtaking Colorado landscape for miles around.

"When I took over the lodge business," she continued, "the biggest problem I saw was lack of clarity. People didn't know what The Grove was anymore, what we stood for, why we were here, or what we had to offer. For example, Dad kept a lot in his head. There were special deals for dozens of guests. Some talked with others and got upset when they realized Richie wasn't giving them the same price. Nothing was written down anywhere." There was no integrity in the system, actually there hadn't really been a system at all. This lack of clarity created confusion, which ultimately created a loss of trust.

"They lost sight of the bigger picture," Sunny said. "That was my biggest challenge when I took the reins of the business. Don't misunderstand me, Ethan, I loved my dad very much. Richie was a good man. He was a man of his word, never cheated anyone, and was always there for me. And you know what? Everyone liked him. But over the years, people had stopped feeling like they could trust him. It made me realize that the question everyone is asking about you isn't 'Do I like you?' It's 'Can I trust you?'" Sunny glanced at her watch.

"Sorry," said Ethan, reaching for his crutches. "You must need to be somewhere. I should start making my way to dinner."

"I'm okay," she said, "I've set up those meetings for you with members of the staff. I think it would help you to have the chance to really dig deep and ask questions." Ethan agreed, marveling at the open way Sunny offered to share all The Grove's best practices. Most corporate environments would never be so transparent.

"Wonderful," she said with a quick glance at the rapidly fading daylight. "But you must be getting tired. Recovering from that kind of injury takes it out of you." Ethan realized she was right. He was exhausted, and his knee was beginning to throb. "Why don't I have room service sent up?"

It was a very welcome idea. He thanked Sunny, but had just one question: "Can you ask Lou if there is any of that ice cream left?"

10
FALSE START

MONDAY MORNING ARRIVED, and with it, a fresh wave of guilt and anxiety. It was one thing to be at a ski resort over the weekend, but the beginning of the work week was completely different. Yesterday, Ethan was an entrepreneur on a weekend vacation. This morning he was the captain of a sinking ship, and he wasn't even on the ship.

The meeting with the 10K team was scheduled for 8:00 AM mountain time, but Ethan had been awake for hours. In fact, he wasn't certain he'd actually been asleep. The realizations he'd had that weekend, once so inspiring, now loomed above him like dark, menacing shadows. Any confidence that he might be able to fix 10K the way Sunny had fixed The Grove had evaporated. All he could think about this morning was the idea that his team had lost faith in him.

His computer was set up at the desk in his new room, videoconference software open and ready to go. He took one deep relaxing breath in through his nose, out through his mouth, and hit connect.

Through his laptop screen, he saw the four members of the 10K executive team seated around that same table back in Minneapolis, all looking at the conference room monitor where his own image was displayed. There were greetings all around, including sympathy about his injured knee and well wishes for his recovery. After a few minutes of catching up, they got down to business.

Things went south from there.

At the close of their Thursday meeting, Ethan had rallied everyone to ramp up their division's tempo. How was it going? He started with Iris, who said they'd had trouble getting materials specs from a few suppliers, but she was working on a fix for that.

"Good," encouraged Ethan. "How are you doing that?" Iris said they were working on better communication with suppliers. When Ethan pressed again, "How?" Iris went on the defensive.

"Don't worry, we'll work it out," she snapped.

Ethan backed off. The team wasn't used to him pressing like this. He moved on to Jenna, to ask about integrating their software with the full range of auto makes and models. She reported that the project was proceeding slowly but smoothly. They were not running up against barriers, but the work was going too slowly to hit the May 1 delivery date. "I have the team working on a new timeline," she said, "and I am pretty confident we can shave some time off."

A corner of Ethan's brain was telling him "abort! abort!" but it was like he had lost control of his own body. Before he could stop himself, he asked again "That's great! How?"

Before Iris had come to tech, she had worked mostly in independent book publishing, which had a much more casual culture than the corporate pressure cooker that Jenna was used to. Jenna's reaction to Ethan's question was to smile reassuringly in a way that conveyed total control of the situation.

"I would be happy to walk you through the plan in our meeting later this morning, Ethan." But she stopped there, and it was clear she would not be elaborating. Somehow Ethan was able to refrain from asking "How?" again for the rest of the meeting.

The videoconference limped on for an eternal fifteen minutes more before mercifully ending, leaving Ethan alone in his room at The Grove, sitting on the edge of his bed with his head in his hands. There was just enough time to hobble to the lobby to acquire a desperately needed infusion of caffeine before his one-on-one with Jenna. He levered himself up onto his crutches and headed toward the door.

The exchange with Iris had surprised him. He knew Sunny's "How?" methodology was new to the team, and he probably should have explained it before diving in headlong, but he hadn't expected outright hostility. And Jenna's cool deferral wasn't much better. Ethan's plan had been to try using some of the things he'd learned so far at The Grove, imagining effortless, generative meetings like he had just seen in the Treehouse. Starting today, he thought he would be the Sunny Bonaventure of 10K. But what if he'd had it all wrong? What if he was more like her dad, Richie?

Back in his room, Ethan logged in to the video call and saw Jenna sitting at her desk, neat and minimalist as ever. After the team meeting this morning, he was not sure how to begin, but luckily Jenna cut right to the heart of the matter.

"Okay, boss. What's going on?" she said with concern. "I know you must be stressed, and I am sure your knee is still bothering you, but it isn't like you to grill folks like that. Is there something else I should know about? Anything I can help with?"

Ethan suddenly felt much more relaxed, relief washing over him. He knew he could always trust Jenna to look for the solution and assume the best in everyone. "I'm so sorry, Jenna—that meeting didn't go at all the way I planned. I've made friends with the owner here, and they have a pretty amazing culture. I've learned a few things and I was trying one of them out. I guess I really stepped in it though."

Ethan noticed Jenna's carefully composed expression and paused. He could tell that he must be failing miserably with regard to the "clarity" pillar he was trying out.

"I'm not quite following," she said carefully. "What, exactly, were you attempting to accomplish?" Ethan could hear the reserve in her voice. He told her about the team meeting in the Treehouse, the relaxed, open communication The Grove team had with each other and with Sunny. He explained Sunny's use of the question "How?" and the way that she asked it repeatedly until she got to a specific action step, complete with a concrete *who* and *when*.

"It seemed like exactly the thing we need to get back on track," he told Jenna, "but I think I have more to learn about using it myself."

"It does sound like a great tool," Jenna said, warming up now that she understood. "But yes, I think perhaps briefing the staff on what you are planning to do might be a good first step. It sounds like the kind of thing you might need to prepare for, especially if you are the one who has to answer."

Yet again Ethan felt like an idiot. What Jenna had said made perfect sense. In hindsight, he couldn't believe he hadn't thought it through. "You are absolutely right, Jenna. If I promise not to subject you to the third degree, can you tell me about the plan you mentioned?" He hoped his tone was conciliatory.

"Definitely," she replied. "But there is one thing I wanted to ask you first. Does that work for you?" Ethan nodded, and Jenna continued. "Last week's meeting made me realize that I don't have much of a handle on our overall direction. I know my projects and at least the status of most of the others. But I just don't know how they all fit together. I've lost track of the strategy. And I think a lot of the others have too."

For a moment Ethan felt defensive. Strategy was his strong suit! It was the reason 10K had been so successful thus far. He thought of the big vision board he had left back in his office—the connections and ideas and innovations drawn in dry erase marker. Seeing that central thread was exactly the thing that made him such a good leader!

But that was just it. Clearly, he was not a great leader at the moment. He had missed a company-wide crisis by a mile. It was obvious that his team didn't trust him. And here was his COO, asking him about their guiding strategy. Then his defensiveness vanished, and Ethan went right back to feeling like he was at the bottom of a mountain—and not the kind with a gondola to fast-track him to the top.

Ethan thought of the meeting in the Treehouse again. Everyone knew the mission, and everyone knew exactly where they were headed. The employees of The Grove would never have needed to ask Sunny the kind of question Jenna had just asked him. They all knew where and how they fit into the organization, and it showed in the ease and confidence of their interactions. Ethan didn't even know what to do next. If Sunny had asked him "How?" right then, he wouldn't have a single answer to give her.

"I just wanted to offer," Jenna continued, "I think sitting down and hammering that strategy out together might go a long way toward hitting our deadline."

In a bit of a daze, Ethan agreed, and Jenna proceeded to walk him through her plan for the software integration. She signed off with well wishes for his recovery. "We're going to get through this, you know that, right?" she asked.

"Right, yes." He put on a smile that he hoped inspired confidence. "Thanks, Jenna. Of course we will."

11
THE HIGHEST STANDARD

THE FIRST MEETING Sunny had set up for Ethan was scheduled for that afternoon. It was with The Grove's director of safety, Bob, the first responder on the mountain Saturday morning as Ethan lay in a humiliated heap. On the heels of his call with Jenna, Ethan felt like the universe was having a real go at him, piling on the humiliation. But Sunny's enthusiasm was reassuring, and Ethan felt like he could use all the help he could get.

All he knew about the man was that Bob was from Tennessee and had spent over a decade in the armed forces, most of that as a Navy Seal. How he ended up at The Grove and what a man of his background was doing here as director of safety for a ski resort were all questions Ethan wanted to ask.

Bob was waiting at the entrance to the gym. To reach the safety office, they wound their way through the gym facility and out to a large garage that housed a stable of snowmobiles, toboggans, and ski equipment. His office consisted of a small cubicle in the far corner of the garage. It was chilly in there; a small space heater gave off just enough heat to sustain life.

"Sorry for the frigid setting," said Bob as the two sat. "My job takes me in and out of here so frequently over the course of the day, it's more uncomfortable to transition between extreme temperatures."

"No problem at all," said Ethan. "I appreciate your making the time to talk with me. I wanted to thank you again for your quick action on the mountain. I found out from the ER doc that my injury could have been much worse had I not been immobilized immediately." Bob nodded appreciatively. Ethan continued, asking about what was involved in being head of safety at The Grove.

Without hesitating, Bob answered, "Number one is the ski patrol team, which, as you saw, patrols the slopes continuously. We also have a doctor and nurse on site during the hours the slopes are open. The ski patrol has excellent resources at their disposal." He also worked closely with the director of grounds to monitor the condition of the slopes as well as the lifts and equipment. "We have an engineering and maintenance team of about a half-dozen employees," he explained. "And I actually work with Chef Lou on food safety as well. Out-of-control bacteria or a failing gondola, either would be devastating, and both are part of my responsibilities."

"That's quite a few plates you have in the air," Ethan said as he ticked the items off on his fingers.

"It is. It takes vigilance," said Bob, "and it takes more than the ability to delegate and a competent team."

Ethan leaned forward. What Bob was talking about hit home. If nothing else, Ethan had already recognized that his style of delegation was not working.

"What do you think of when I say 'Special Ops'?" Bob asked.

"That you could kill me fourteen ways before I could sneeze?" The corners of Bob's eyes twitched. It took Ethan a moment to recognize this as a smile.

"It's tough to make Ranger, SEAL, MARSOC, or any of the Special Ops teams," said Bob. "Only a small minority make the cut, and the single trait they have in common is neither natural athleticism nor strength. It's not a skill set or even endurance. It's this: **An extreme desire to learn and improve. At everything.**" The SEAL creed, Bob explained, is: "The lives of my teammates and the success of our mission depend on me— my technical skill, tactical proficiency, and attention to detail. My training is never complete."

Heavy, thought Ethan, shivering a bit in the cold garage.

"The training never stops," Bob continued. "That mind-set is what I bring to The Grove. My core motivation, you could say, is the assurance of competency itself. It's another of our 8 Pillars, and of all eight, competency is probably the one I focus on most." The men sat in silence for a moment. Outside in the distance Ethan could just hear what sounded like a beginner ski lesson starting out. "Let me ask you this, Mr. Parker: Which doctor would you trust more to operate on that knee, the one who's constantly learning about the cutting-edge research, or the one who stops researching on their last day of medical school?" Bob didn't expect an answer. "Every day I ask myself: What do you know how to do today that you had no idea about a year ago? If I don't have three or four answers rolling off my tongue without thinking, then I'm in trouble."

Ethan's mind was spinning. Bob was talking about things that seemed detached from the everyday mechanics of the workplace. Ethan had expected something along the lines of rigid performance metrics and meticulous tracking systems.

"Another aspect of my role here is that I help encourage **COMPETENCY** throughout our staff," Bob said. "When I got here, I implemented a staff development program. Within one year, the lodge's net profit rose by more than 20 percent. We did this through three core initiatives."

Bob explained how he worked to create this culture of competency. "Every staff member of The Grove reads, no matter if they have advanced degrees or no degree at all. We invest in hundreds of books that help employees grow, stretch, and develop their skills." He described The Grove as having a reading culture.

Based on what Ethan had seen in the Great Room and the Reading Room, he believed it. In the end table drawer by his bed, along with the customary Gideon Bible, Ethan had noticed three books, all of which he remembered reading when he was younger: *The Walking Drum*, *The Old Man and the Sea*, and *The Hobbit*. He mentioned the discovery of those books to Bob.

"Those are three of my all-time favorites," Bob said, nodding. "I believe that our guests come here looking for some type of adventure. Our mission says we give people a 'mountain experience,' and to me, that means adventure. Each of those books is a classic adventure of the human spirit, and we place books like this in every guest room."

Next, Bob introduced the second core initiative he implemented at The Grove. "We also have a learning program called mastermind groups, and every employee belongs to one of these learning groups. We want learning to feel like a team sport. There are two types of mastermind groups: one where everyone is from the same branch, and another where each member is from a different branch of the organization." This structure, Bob explained, sharpens people, supports their growth, and creates friendships and synergy. "The whole is greater than the sum of its parts," he said.

When Bob discussed the third core initiative with Ethan, his tone became quite serious. "Our people believe in mentorship, and everyone on staff has a mentor and is a mentor at all times," he said.

What a hard initiative to get off the ground, Ethan thought. It was difficult for him to imagine.

"We don't have a formal system of performance reviews," Bob continued, "but we've realized that people actually crave real feedback; they want to know where they stand. Doing that through an impersonal and stressful performance review system just didn't fit with the culture here. In the context of a supportive relationship with a mentor, it's possible to make sure everyone gets the constructive feedback that will help them improve." For example, right now Bob was mentoring Milo. "Just a teenager, but what a sharp kid!"

Ethan told Bob what the surgeon had said, about how lucky he was that Milo had been right there at the scene of the accident, and how Milo's quick action on the slope had saved his knee from further damage, a tricky surgery, and a much tougher recovery.

Bob nodded. "She's right, but that wasn't luck. It was competency on display. I am very proud of him." The skin around Bob's eyes wrinkled.

COMPASSION

12
WHEN IT'S DARKEST

BACK IN HIS ROOM, Ethan was regretting scheduling three calls in one day. After the meeting with the whole 10K team and the follow-up call with Jenna, he wasn't sure he had the presence of mind to pull off another one-on-one. The conversation with Bob had helped a little, but as the afternoon wound down, Ethan found himself wishing he had scheduled his call with Dom for the next morning. But what was done was done, so Ethan clicked "connect," and the view of his CTO sitting in his Minneapolis office blinked into view.

"Hey boss. How's the knee?"

Ethan replied with the usual reassurances—his knee really did feel much better today—and the comfortable rapport he had with Dom took the edge off his anxiety. They chatted about the status of Dom's division and their progress toward the deadline, which seemed to be going well. Ethan had decided there would be no more surprise trust tactics like his disastrous "How?" experiment, and that the best thing he could do right now was listen and support the team. This seemed to be going well until Dom was wrapping things up.

"I just have one more issue I wanted to raise with you, Ethan," Dom said. "It's a little sensitive, and I don't want to sound like a jerk, but I'm having some serious second thoughts about Jenna."

Ethan was instantly back on edge. Like everything else at 10K, this felt like it was coming out of nowhere. "What's going on?" he asked cautiously, bracing himself.

"Well, I mean, she's the COO. She's supposed to have the pulse of the whole organization. I'm concerned that she didn't bring any of this to your attention. To be frank, I was more surprised at how surprised you were than I was about the company's status last week."

Ethan thought about everything he knew of Dom and Jenna's interactions over the years since Jenna had joined 10K. They had always worked well together, even if they were not particularly close. He remembered Dom had a few reservations when Ethan brought her on, but she had, in his opinion, more than proven her value.

Dom continued: "You know, I just wonder if her lack of experience might be holding her back." That was it—now he remembered—Dom had felt she was too young, too inexperienced. Ethan knew he would have to treat this situation carefully. He would have to remain neutral, though he had always felt that Jenna's performance was exemplary on all counts. Clearly Dom had his own opinion.

"I appreciate your candor," Ethan started, falling back on some standard office speak. He didn't want to discount Dom's opinion, but he couldn't say he agreed. Especially when just this morning, it had been Jenna questioning his own leadership skills!

"I can tell you that in my call with Jenna earlier today she and I talked about all our active projects," Ethan said. "I felt like she had a pretty good handle on their status. If anyone has lost track of things, Dom, I think the buck stops with me." It was a hard pill to swallow. Admitting something like that would have been a lot harder for Ethan even just a few days ago. But for some reason today he didn't feel any internal resistance. Maybe after the fall down the mountain and the seemingly unending parade of disastrous meetings with his team, he'd just been worn down.

"Well, that's a generous position of you to take," Dom replied, sounding unconvinced. "If you think she has things under control, I'll take your word. Don't get me wrong—I like Jenna. She is a great colleague and very effective in a lot of ways. I'd just feel better if I knew the COO could see down the pipeline."

Suddenly what Sunny had said to Ethan in the Treehouse flashed through his mind: What people are asking about you isn't "Do I like you?" It's "Can I trust you?" He was beginning to see what she meant.

Dom and Ethan signed off, and Ethan leaned as far back as the chair would let him. The rabbit hole just kept getting deeper and deeper. Not only did it seem like his team did not trust him, now it looked like they might not trust each other. His first attempt at using some of The Grove's culture building had crashed and burned, and he was still combing through the wreckage, finding even more problems. When was it going to end?

After a call with his wife, Maya, to check in and reassure her that his knee seemed to be healing well, Ethan made his way down to the restaurant. It was getting late, and he didn't have much of an appetite, but he was vaguely curious about whether there was any of that ice cream left over. He noticed Milo sitting at the bar, enthusiastically scarfing down a huge plate of pasta. He looked like he had just come in from the slopes.

Ethan sat down beside the teenager. "Another day out skiing? Shouldn't you be in school or something?"

Milo grinned. "Oh don't worry about that. I was at school all day. I like to do the evening Ski Patrol sweep. It's a great way to clear my head in the evenings. How are you doing, Mr. Parker? Recovery going ok? You look pretty tired."

Ethan laughed at the refreshing teenage candor. "I am that, Milo. You know, Sunny Bonaventure really has built an amazing place here. It seems like she has everything under control."

"She certainly does!" said Milo, before taking another bite. "Mom's pretty awesome. Growing up here was like being part of a huge extended family. I always knew I could rely on anyone at the lodge whenever I needed anything."

Mom? Ethan blinked. Suddenly Milo's late-night presence at the restaurant bar made much more sense. "That sounds wonderful. I had a big family growing up. It's great to have so many people watching out for you. I wish I could bring some of that feeling into my own company, but it feels like an uphill battle."

The server, Sarah, came over and Ethan's tentative request for more of the cookies and ice cream was met with an indulgent smile. "We've got plenty—don't you worry," she said. "Lou thought you might be down for more!"

Marveling, Ethan turned to Milo. "So what's your take? How does your mom do it? Encourage such an amazing culture? I could really use some of her magic."

Milo had just about scraped his plate clean. "I think it really has to do with how dedicated everyone is here. Most folks who work here feel like it's an extended family—my experience isn't because my mom owns the place. Everyone feels like I do."

Ethan nodded. "Got it. It's about how loyal your employees are to the operation."

Milo raised an eyebrow. "Actually," he said, "it's the other way around. It's about how loyal The Grove is to the employees. Mom takes that 8 Pillar thing really seriously. I think she feels that she has the biggest responsibility of all to treat the staff with real compassion."

"Huh," said Ethan. "Like benefits, you mean?"

Milo shrugged. "That's a part of it. Health insurance and stuff was already decent, though. Grandpa Richie never got rid of those. Mom wanted to go farther. She wanted every employee to know how much she cared about them, how she had their back." He explained that when his mom was working in San Francisco, she had a lot of artist friends who were trying to make it, starting at the bottom of the ladder. Sunny knew how hard it could be, so she started an emergency fund for employees. It was used for short-term housing issues, health emergencies, or personal crises such as getting away from an abusive partner or getting out from under drugs or alcohol.

Ethan thought about the young man Jamie, whom Chef Lou had mentioned in the meeting in the Treehouse, and how the group celebrated his six months of sobriety.

"But it's not just money," Milo continued. "Just helping people find good housing is a big thing. She will literally help people find an apartment! And everyone here is always learning—there's lots of on-the-job training. Plenty of people work their way up or they even go on to opportunities elsewhere—things they never could have done without the training they got here."

Ethan was impressed with Milo's level of engagement. When he was Milo's age, his main concern was getting his hands on the latest Nintendo game. "What's the biggest single factor, would you say?" he asked Milo.

"She just makes people feel appreciated. Mom always says you can't fake it," Milo said. "It's more than programs and policies; it's about having actual compassion for people. It's about noticing stuff. You know, really seeing people. That's her secret."

Ethan sat back feeling a little sentimental. He couldn't help thinking about his impending parenthood. He hoped he and Maya could do half as good a job as Milo's parents had. A fifteen-year-old who understood **COMPASSION** this well would be an achievement he and Maya would be immensely proud of.

"Well," Milo said, scraping his plate of the last bits of sauce. "Time for homework. It was great to see you, Mr. Parker! I'm sure you will do great with your problems at work. It'll all work out in the end. Have a good night!"

Just as Milo headed out, Sarah returned with Ethan's dessert. He sat there, enjoying the dish just as much as the first time around. After the day he'd had, it was a welcome moment of calm. Everything was falling down around him, but for the first time since that disastrous meeting on Thursday, Ethan felt that no matter how bad things got, there might just be a way through.

13
HOW?

ETHAN SLEPT UNTIL a luxurious 9:30 the next morning. His mother had always said that if you slept late, it was because your body needed it, and he wanted his healing muscles and tendons to have all the resources he could give them. His meeting with the next Grove staff member was not until later in the afternoon. As he savored his coffee and a delicious bagel piled high with lox and cream cheese in the Great Room, he thought through everything he had seen so far at The Grove. After a few days, he could see exactly what Milo had meant last night. There was a sense of connectedness and camaraderie he had never encountered in such a big workplace. In fact, it felt a lot more like a college sports team instead of a typical workplace. It was clear that everyone who worked at The Grove knew they could rely on everyone else, no matter what they might need.

Sunny's comment about building a trustworthy business hadn't really made sense to Ethan when she first said it. His interpretation of a "trustworthy business" was one that delivered on its promises and where employees were honest with each other.

But he was beginning to see the broader implications of the idea. What if it was all about employees knowing, without ever having to ask, that they could all rely on each other? It would explain why things at 10K were so broken. No one had lied. No one had broken anyone's confidence. But certainly there was a widespread feeling of disconnection. If Ethan hadn't seen that clearly enough last week, his call with Dom yesterday left no room for doubt. Ethan's team didn't trust him, and apparently they didn't trust each other either.

So what was the way through? The disastrous "How?" experiment had left him feeling reticent to implement ideas from The Grove without learning more about them. If there had been a specific instance of dishonesty, it would be straightforward enough to address. But Ethan still didn't quite understand how to go about fixing a problem that was so difficult to pin down. He looked up from his musings to see Sunny herself walking across the lobby toward him.

"You know, if I can't be out on the slopes," she said, sitting down next to him, "I do think sitting in front of a blazing fire is an absolutely acceptable substitute." He had chosen a seat in front of one of the huge fireplaces, and he had to agree with her.

"I wanted to check on you and see what you've thought about our ideas so far. I know you met with Bob yesterday, and Milo told me all about your chat last night at dinner. I'm always curious to hear what people think of how we do things here. You've provided me with a perfect test case!"

Ethan set his mug down and leaned forward. It seemed like a great opportunity to ask Sunny her own million-dollar question. "It's been really enlightening so far. I've been blown away by everything I've heard, and I think I'm beginning to see what you mean by a 'trustworthy organization.'" Ethan paused, but after an encouraging nod from Sunny, he continued. "I would love to be able to replicate what you've done here at my own company. But it just seems like such a huge undertaking. It's amazing how seamless everything is, but I can't really see what's driving it. It doesn't seem to be one thing or another, it's just, well, everywhere. So the question I have, really, is . . . " he paused for a moment and looked at Sunny with a shrug, "How?"

Sunny threw back her head and laughed, and Ethan did too. He hadn't meant to make a joke, but Sunny's reaction put him at ease.

"An excellent question!" she said, still beaming. "One of my favorites. There really isn't one answer. There are hundreds. When you do the 'How?' exercise, both you and the other person need to be working together, looking for an answer that's concrete and specific. You don't stop until you find an action step that can be done today or tomorrow at the latest, so let's see if we can get to that answer together." Sunny explained that doing this every day, over and over, resulted in The Grove's culture of awareness. "This culture facilitates clearly defined, achievable short-term goals; it creates the kind of trust that permeates every aspect of the business because you get clarity, which builds trust."

If the only way to build a trustworthy culture was this long-term, multifaceted approach, wondered Ethan, what chance did he have of fixing 10K in four months? Feeling discouraged, he asked the only question he could think of. "How?"

Sunny gave him an approving look. "When you are first starting out, you need to go through four key stages. We sort of stumbled our way through them when I was trying to bring my grandfather's values back to the lodge. Since it was a learn-as-you-go situation, it took us a long time, and there were many fits and starts. But once we realized we had created something truly unique, we reverse-engineered the process."

The first stage, Sunny explained, is to *confront the unvarnished reality* of the situation. "It's what I mean when I say 'nothing is a sales or accountability problem; it's all a trust problem.' Realizing that the problem is really a trust problem is sometimes the biggest hurdle."

"Well," said Ethan, "I've certainly got that covered! I've been confronting reality all week, and the layers keep getting deeper." He knew that 10K was in trouble, and he'd started to see where all the breakdowns in trust had been hovering just below the surface.

"Then you are probably already into stage two," replied Sunny. "The second stage is to *identify the root cause* of each one of your main issues. If you thought you had a leadership problem— go deeper. Since everything is really a trust problem, ask yourself where, in the context of your leadership, did trust initially break down?" She said that the 8 Pillars were necessary for stage two. Ultimately, the core issue was always related to one of the pillars.

Ethan thought about this in the context of the problems he had already identified. What was at the root of his communication and accountability problems? Even harder to think about was what might be behind the leadership issue.

"The third stage," Sunny continued, "is to *create a common language*. This unifies teams and gives them the chance to solve the real issue on common ground and with solid communication. Talking through the 8 Pillars gives you a way to look at your so-called leadership problem, and it will help you to identify where that trust breakdown has happened. It allows you to get really specific."

Ethan was feeling good about the steps Sunny was outlining. He'd already realized he had a clarity problem, not a leadership problem. He was also pretty sure that 10K had a connection problem rather than the communication problem he initially diagnosed during Thursday's difficult meeting. "All right," he said. "I am with you on all of this, and I think I have actually experienced a few of these stages already this week. So, what comes next, and how do I fix it?"

"Fixing it is the fourth stage," Sunny said. "This is where you *implement a system of tools and strategies* that are targeted directly at the problems you have identified. These strategies must be specific and concrete. This is the long game, but there are some strategies that will start rebuilding trust almost immediately. Focus on those first, but start to build the long-term habits too."

Sunny explained that if 10K was struggling with connection, there were team-building exercises that could help the team members understand each other better. Those often had immediate results. And if a leadership issue was actually a clarity issue, it would be necessary to learn better ways of asking questions and presenting data. "Trust is built on a foundation of these little things," she said, "done consistently, over and over again. And you have to accept that there will be bumps in the road. Everything you try might not work the first time. The critical thing is to keep trying. Every day holds a hundred new opportunities to build trust."

Ethan was beginning to feel hopeful again. This seemed doable. "So you have a second chance at these things?" He asked, thinking of his botched "How?" attempt. "It seems almost like everything could be an opportunity to build trust when you think about it this way."

"Absolutely," Sunny said. "Trust is a learnable skill set. It's not something you just 'have'; it's not something unchangeable, something that only some people have and others don't. Trust is action. You can be learning and practicing it anytime, anywhere. My grandfather somehow knew these things intuitively. He had a knack for trust building and did it naturally. But that sense of trustworthiness was not limited to him. Everyone who worked for him learned from his example, and the skills for building trust permeated the whole culture."

Ethan marveled at Sunny's wisdom. "How did you figure all of this out? And if trust had degraded so badly, how were you able to see the way to fixing things?" He'd finished his breakfast by now, but Ethan was too dialed in to the conversation to notice.

"I think it was actually because I left and came back," Sunny said. "I was gone for a long time, and the difference was much clearer to me than to people who had experienced my father's ill-advised changes incrementally. I had very clear memories from my youth of my grandfather's way of running things. There was such a stark contrast, comparing those memories to the situation I found when I came home." Ethan thought about the contrast between what he was seeing at The Grove and the state of things at 10K, and he could see what Sunny meant.

"Don't get me wrong," she added. "It wasn't easy. I got a lot more wrong than I got right at first. Asking yourself these questions—how you can have compassion in an interaction, or how to build systems that encourage contribution and results—can be easy; but answering those questions can be challenging. I've found that the results leave no room for argument. When trust increases, productivity increases. Output increases, innovation, loyalty, revenue—everything."

"Right," said Ethan, thinking of the sign in the lobby: "Trust is everything."

14
CRISIS RESPONSE

ALTHOUGH HE WAS FEELING worlds better about the future, Ethan still couldn't help but think that there was something more specific he was going to need. He wanted to ask Sunny one last "How?" According to her own methods, Ethan still had not gotten to a concrete action he could take today or tomorrow, with a who, what, and a when. 10K's current predicament needed an immediate intervention, and even implementing the four stages were just a tad too big picture. He had become increasingly comfortable around Sunny, and although he didn't want to offend her by pushing back on her methodology, Ethan had the sense that she would be open to just about any question he could think up. He decided to share specifics about what was happening at 10K.

"The reality is," he said hesitantly, "we're in a full-blown crisis. It's not just a rough patch with a few things going wrong. With absolutely no warning, I've found myself looking at the very real possibility of the whole company collapsing in a matter of months." Ethan stopped for a moment, surprised at his own candor. Admitting the extent of the issues was one thing with his friends, but it was different with a newer acquaintance, especially someone as successful as Sunny. But he forced himself to continue. "My problem is so big, if I don't fix it right away, we won't even be around long enough for people to build better connection with each other, or for my employees to see me making and keeping commitments over and over again." He paused, bracing himself to ask this final, critical "How": "How would you handle a complete and utter emergency?"

"Ah," Sunny replied. "Yes, a crisis definitely demands a specific and targeted response. I think I understand a little better what you've been looking for! Luckily, we've faced quite a few situations of that magnitude. In fact, what we've realized is that crisis is an absolutely inevitable part of running any business."

Quite a few? The idea of facing another disaster like the one he was in made Ethan's stomach turn. He must not have done a good job hiding his reaction, because Sunny elaborated: "Even if you have created the greatest and most efficient system on the planet, there will always be some external situation that can bring you to your knees. Being prepared for a crisis is not overpreparation—it is a necessity. When The Grove faced its first crisis after I took over, it was our COO at the time, Onika Wallace, who led us through it. She helped us develop the capacity for responding to other crisis events in the future. Ultimately, what we discovered is good news for you: Your fastest opportunity to build trust is in a crisis."

"Is Ms. Wallace looking for a job at a small tech startup in Minneapolis?" Ethan ask wryly. "Because I know someone who'd love to hire her yesterday."

Sunny got the joke. "She's actually running her own company out in Los Angeles. But I can teach you what she taught us." Onika had enlisted in the coast guard straight out of high school, though by the time she came to The Grove she had gotten her MBA and worked in the private sector for many years. "For sailors on the open water, often deployed in crisis situations, knowing how to respond in those moments means life or death. Now, we're not dealing with life or death most of the time, but the possibility of ski accidents means that we do have to be prepared for that eventuality," Sunny said. "This way of thinking could be applied to any crisis, and Onika built a level of resiliency into The Grove's operations that saved the organization time and time again." Ethan leaned in, wishing he had some way to take notes.

Sunny waved a server over for a coffee refill. "When we have any sort of crisis here," she said, "the first thing we do is pause. This is critical. Without a pause to assess the situation, you can't hope to find your way out of it. Next, we ask two questions. The first is 'What can I control?' with the emphasis on *can*. Most people's first instinct in a crisis is to look at what went wrong, what caused the crisis."

Ethan could relate to that instinct, thinking of his first reaction to the dreadful Thursday meeting with his team. He admitted that the first question he'd asked himself, on the phone with Maya, was "Where did we go wrong?"

"But that question should always be saved for later," Sunny explained. "In the moment, you should be looking to identify what you have direct control over. Most people get distracted by thoughts about what they can't do, the obstacles. But that wastes precious brainpower when you are dealing with an emergency. There's always more you can control than it seems at first." She further clarified the point: "Finally, we ask, 'What can I do right now?' Once you have identified what you can control, it's easier to see opportunities for action that will get you back on track. When you are truly in a crisis, it's essential to narrow your focus to one single priority. Even two priorities is too many."

Ethan couldn't tell whether this was great news or terrible news. "Just one?" he asked. "I'm not sure there is just one priority—in fact, I'm pretty sure the whole root of the crisis is that *everything* is falling apart at once. Don't get me wrong, focusing on only one thing is exactly what I want to do, but I'm afraid if I do, whatever I am *not* focused on will bite us from behind."

Sunny got it. This was a real fear, but as she explained it: "That is exactly why you need only one priority—in a crisis there are always too many things to do, and too many things breaking down. What defines 'crisis' is that everything is legitimately an emergency. That's exactly why you have to narrow your focus."

Ethan was not convinced yet. Meeting 10K's deadline was their one priority, but in order to do that, there were hundreds of other things that had to happen. "But how do you choose? And what about everything that you don't choose? How do you make sure it all gets done?"

"In a way, you don't," Sunny said. "The goal in a crisis becomes 'get through it' not 'get everything done.' A crisis demands a different way of looking at strategy. Your single priority should be something you can do right away, but then you repeat the process and ask the two questions again. You handle one priority at a time, then move on to the next one. But it's still important to consider just one at a time."

It seemed a bit paradoxical to Ethan, but Sunny explained that the two main benefits of focusing on just one priority were (1) to keep a group from getting distracted, and (2) to make sure things got done completely. "In a crisis," she assured, "fully completing tasks is the key benchmark."

"Okay, but how do you do this with a team?" he asked, already thinking about building a plan. "Does everyone work on the same priority?"

"Yes and no," Sunny answered.

Again with the paradoxes, thought Ethan.

"The team should have one priority," she clarified, "but each individual should have their own single priority that directly supports the main priority. And everyone's individual priority should be just as immediate and completable. Timelines become compressed, and everything must stay flexible, which is why you need to work only on these short goals."

Sunny was clearly a pro with crisis management. Ethan was curious to hear how she and The Grove had weathered these storms. "Another hallmark of a crisis is that things change rapidly—within a twenty-four-hour period sometimes. You need to maintain agility—even the ability to change that one priority at the drop of a hat, if the scenario changes. Of course, you do want to be looking at least a little ahead. Most strategic plans are designed to be quarterly, annually, or even longer. But in a crisis you want to work in one week blocks. Don't lose sight of the long-term plan, but a crisis priority should span days or at most, a week."

This, Ethan thought, *cinches it. This is exactly what 10K needs.* He had one final question though. "You know, this is the first conversation we've had where you didn't reference the 8 Pillars. Do they come in here too?" He couldn't imagine that the pillars would be absent.

"Of course!" she said. "The single priority focus goes for the 8 Pillars as well. Any one of them can be employed in a crisis, but you should choose the one pillar you think will have the greatest impact and focus on that. A good one for almost any situation is clarity. No matter the situation, clarity increases trust instantly." Sunny went on: "You should also be applying a clarity lens to your external communication, as well as internal. Even private client emails, for example, are an opportunity to sharpen clarity. Crisis situations are often the result of external factors or demands, so focusing on the external manifestation of the pillars is just as important, and sometimes more so."

Ethan thought about it. 10K didn't have customers or much marketing yet, but they certainly had stakeholders. Very important stakeholders. Stakeholders with purse strings. He wanted to think more about what 10K's one priority might be, but he needed to check in with Maya before his next meeting. He thanked Sunny for her time and headed back up to his room, excited to tell Maya about everything he was learning.

CHARACTER

15
A MEASURE OF INTEGRITY

THAT AFTERNOON, Ethan was scheduled to meet with Amirah Clark, the director of finance. In the lobby, along with the usual directory of services, maps of the lodge and slopes, and pamphlets for other local attractions, Ethan had found a little booklet about The Grove that featured head shots and brief biographical sketches of the leadership team. While he finished his lunch, he read up on her background.

Amirah was from Abilene, Texas, went to school in Houston, and was eventually head-hunted onto the staff of a large Wall Street firm. After more than a decade, she left New York City and took her current position at The Grove. It was puzzling to him why Amirah would toss out a promising career in the financial capital of the world to run the books at a little Colorado ski resort. Another odd fact stuck out to Ethan. Before taking her master's in accounting and going into the world of corporate finance, Amirah went to seminary. Theology to finance seemed like a pretty radical leap.

Ethan took the elevator up to the second floor and crutched his way down a hallway. He found the suite number and paused for breath. The door was ajar; he knocked lightly.

"Door's open," a voice called out from inside. "You can come right in!"

Ethan poked his head in the doorway. Everything in the place gave a sense of simplicity. There was a clean glass-top desk, and black-and-white nature photos dotted the white walls. In the center of the room, two small, white leather couches flanked a coffee table.

"Please," said Amirah, gesturing to one of the couches. "Have a seat."

Ethan sat down, grateful for the comfortable setting. "Thanks so much for taking the time to talk with me," he said. He still couldn't quite believe how helpful everyone had been, and Amirah seemed to be no exception. "I read your bio," he said, as she took a seat on the other couch. "I have to say, it's quite impressive. I was curious, though, if you don't mind my asking . . ."

"Please," she said.

"What made you switch your studies, from theology to finance?"

Amirah put her hands together in thought, touching her fingertips to her chin as she considered her reply. "I love theology. My dad was a pastor, and my faith is important to me. But my God-given gift is numbers," she said. "I've always loved numbers. Numbers tell the truth. They don't lie. I went into finance, I guess you could say, because I thought accounting could keep people honest."

She clasped her hands together on her lap and leaned back into her chair. "I spent a decade on Wall Street, where I learned that people find all sorts of ways to justify, bend the rules, twist the meaning, and yes, even change the actual numbers and interpret them to serve their own ends." Amirah had always seen finance as a necessary part of doing business, but eventually she realized that, more than anything else, finance revealed character. "Sometimes that's not a lovely revelation," she said. "In fact, after my first decade in the industry, I almost quit and went back to seminary!"

She paused and took a sip of water. "That's when I got a call from Chef Lou."

Aha, thought Ethan, *a New York connection.* "Really," he said. "Forgive my asking, but coming from the high-stakes world of a big Wall Street firm, wasn't the work here a little . . . "

"Boring?" she filled in the blank.

Ethan hesitated. He hadn't meant to offend. "I guess I was going to say . . . not that challenging?"

"Actually, it was fascinating!" Amirah countered, leaning forward onto her elbows. "The financials were already in decent shape. Not perfect, but decent. Putting all that in order was simple. The interesting part was setting up a company-wide accountability system."

"Like performance reviews?" Ethan asked.

"I'm not interested in measuring performance the way many companies do," Amirah explained, shaking her head. "The way Sunny runs things, that more or less takes care of itself. My job was to set up a way to measure and motivate **CHARACTER**."

Ah, the pillars again, Ethan thought. "But how in the world do you measure character?"

"It's actually easier than you might think. You ask."

Ethan waited for Amirah to say more, then realized she'd completed her statement. "That's it? You ask? You're going to have to help me see that."

She brought her fingertips to her chin again as she considered her next words. "Most people have a natural sense of what's right and what's wrong. And for the most part, especially within the same cultural context, your idea of right and wrong and my idea of right and wrong will match about ninety percent of the time."

Ethan gave her a dubious look.

"What you need to consider is everything we agree on," Amirah began. "Most ethics conversations focus on the few places we don't. For example, most people would agree that it's bad to push a grandma in front of a train, and it's good to help someone who is in distress, et cetera. As much as ethics philosophers love to debate it, most of us are not going to be faced with the trolly problem in our everyday lives." She explained that when it comes to character, the hiring process is crucial. Hiring managers and leaders need to define what they mean by character, so the goals are consistent across the organization. "But it can't stop there. Even when you hire people of basically good character, you can't assume perfection."

Amirah's philosophy was simple: Most people have an innate sense of right and wrong but need to exercise the muscle. Also, situations get complicated, so having a yardstick everyone could agree on is critical. "Here at The Grove," she said "our yardstick is our mission. We firmly believe we should always do the right thing for the guest, for the staff, for the lodge, and for the mountain."

As the director of finance, Amirah asked her team, once per quarter, just four questions. "Over the past ninety days," she explained to Ethan, "on a scale of one to ten, how consistent have you been at doing the right thing for each guest? for the staff? for The Grove itself? for the mountain? My favorite definition of character is the one I learned from my father: 'Character is what you do when no one is looking.' I share this with my small team and ask them about it from time to time."

It was one of the strangest, most radical approaches to management Ethan had ever heard, although he was beginning to get used to that the longer he stayed at The Grove. "And what do you do with their answers?"

"The rankings themselves are not all that important," said Amirah. "The real point is where it goes from there. The reflections and discussion that follow are where the rubber meets the road."

Ethan tried to imagine the kinds of conversations that would emerge with his team at 10K if he tried this approach. "Have you ever had anyone rate themselves with all tens?"

"Not so far," she said, chuckling softly. "If we did, I'd probably assume I had done a poor job in the hiring process. People of good character aren't likely to rate themselves as perfect."

"That sounds awfully trusting," mused Ethan.

"Bingo," Amirah said, with a subtle nod.

"Doesn't this all seem a long way off the path from the responsibilities of an ordinary director of finance?"

Amirah smiled. "Yes and no. Here's something else I observed in the corporate world, and it's something they most definitely do not teach in business school: A lack of trust is your single biggest expense. When trust goes down, every metric starts moving—in the wrong direction. Time. Money. Customer loyalty. Retention. Reputation. The lower the trust, the more time everything takes, the more everything costs, and the lower the loyalty of everyone involved. The fastest way to go extinct is to lose trust!"

This made sense to Ethan, and he listened intently as Amirah spoke. "Another responsibility of leaders is making sure that they are not systemizing against the very character they say they want to have. For example, some organizations incentivize salespeople to have low character simply through their bonus structures." Amirah added: "I grew up a few miles outside a tiny town in Taylor County, miles from Abilene. Every day I'd take the bus home from school and see my neighbor's fruit and veggie stand sitting there at the end of his dirt driveway. There, next to the produce, right near the berries, tomatoes, and sweet corn, sat a tin pail with money sticking out of it. There were ones, fives, tens, and loose change in the bottom, but no farmer, no teenage worker, and no hired hand in sight. You know who worked the stand?"

"The kids?" guessed Ethan.

Amirah shook her head. "Nobody, that's who. Not a living soul. Instead, there was a little handwritten sign that read: *Pick what you want, pay what you owe.* Mr. Olson ran that little produce stand on the honor system. People were expected to make their own change. And you know what? They did!"

When she was a kid, she hadn't thought much about it, but once she had made it on Wall Street, Amirah thought about this a lot. "What efficiency! He saved money because he didn't have to hire anyone to sit there and watch the till. He saved time because he didn't have to be there. And he built a level of customer loyalty that was off the charts. But one night, Mr. Olson's barn caught on fire. The fire department got there as soon as they could, but they were too late. It was already all over."

"Ouch," said Ethan.

"Not ouch," said Amirah, shaking her head again. "The fire was already out by the time the fire department arrived. The neighbors saw the flames, showed up in minutes, and hosed and bucket-brigaded that thing into submission. By the time the two fire trucks arrived, there wasn't a hot spark to be found."

Amazing, thought Ethan, but that wasn't the end of Amirah's story. "My neighbor trusted his customers to do the right thing—and they had his back," she said. "You know what else? Along with that high character, he made very solid profits. Trust kept that business going for many decades!"

16
SOMETHING NEW

THE CALL WITH IRIS, 10K's lead UX designer, was scheduled for 3:00, and after his last few meetings with The Grove's leadership team, Ethan felt much more confident about everything he was learning. A week ago, he would have dragged his feet and dreaded this call. After his wipeout with "How?," upsetting Iris in front of everyone, the last thing he should have been looking forward to was this next conversation with her. Yet here he was, back in his room at The Grove, excitedly waiting for the call to begin.

The screen blinked into view, and he saw Iris sitting in her office, the view of the Minneapolis skyline visible out her window. Without any delay, Ethan launched straight into the speech he had prepared that morning over what had probably been too much coffee. "Iris, I wanted to start off with a sincere apology for putting you on the spot the other day," he began. "I didn't mean to subject you to the third degree, and it was entirely unacceptable. I want to let you know that I deeply value your contributions to 10K and I am sorry if I made you feel otherwise." It looked to Ethan as if Iris relaxed at least a little bit.

"Thanks Ethan—I appreciate that," she said. "Jenna did mention something to me about a new management technique that you were trying out?"

Her mention of "management technique" made him think of Sunny's dad Richie and his failed approaches. Ethan winced a bit—that was the last thing he wanted. "Not a management technique exactly. It isn't really important right now—I completely mangled it anyway. What I really want to do on this call is give you a chance to ask questions and tell me where your projects stand. Wherever they are, I won't hang up until we have a working plan. I want you to know you have my full support!"

Iris blinked a few times and then looked down at her desk. She seemed to be struggling with what she wanted to say next. "There is actually something I needed to talk to you about. It's about the client. I think I work with them more closely than anyone else at 10K." She paused, searching for words. "I have a few meetings with them scheduled for next week, and I'm worried about what to tell them. If we are this behind, I am not sure I can just go along like we're on schedule."

Last week Ethan would probably have crumbled at this. Losing the client's trust would mean losing the client, and 10K with it. He could add "external trust problem" to his ever-growing list. Instead, he took a deep breath and reminded himself of Sunny's coaching yesterday: Trust is a learnable skill set. And Iris had felt like she could bring this up with him, which was an improvement on last week as well. He wanted to emphasize his appreciation for her willingness to speak up. After all, Iris had been the one who rated the prospects for meeting the deadline at "three." It was Iris who had the courage to face up to the reality of their situation, and here she was again, willing to stare reality in the face. Ethan was suddenly very grateful he had hired her.

"Thank you for trusting me with this, Iris," he said, sitting up a little straighter. "I'm really glad you felt you could bring it up. I want to make sure you know that I am here for you, and

I am willing to do whatever needs to be done." He sounded a little wooden, even to himself, but he figured it was better to try, even if he hadn't quite nailed the delivery yet. And it did seem to have a positive impact on Iris. What she said next came out in a nervous rush.

"I don't want to say anything out of line here, but I feel like I am getting mixed messages from the other team members," she said. "I don't know what to tell the client. I need to have a consistent set of data and right now I just don't."

Ethan thought of his earlier conversations with Jenna and Dom. If the team members had lost trust in each other, maybe it was due to a lack of clarity. That seemed to be a major focus for Sunny as a leader, and Ethan could certainly see why. Thinking of the clarity pillar, he asked Iris for specifics about her project and where she thought the others' were. Maybe if he could get clarity from everyone, he'd be able to help them all chart a path forward.

As Iris explained the different aspects of the UX development, the tension seemed to ease out of the conversation. Ethan listened intently, taking notes for later. He wanted to make sure he would remember everything correctly. There were a few discrepancies with Dom and Jenna's reports once Iris started explaining the overlaps, and Ethan noted those as well. He was beginning to get a better picture of everything, which made him feel more confident about possibilities for repair.

As the conversation went on, Ethan made sure to think about Sunny's questions—he wanted to make sure that he took every chance he had to try to build trust. Was he being compassionate? Was he taking enough notes to be sure of his ability to be clear later on? Ethan had always tried to be a good boss, one that he hoped his employees liked. But with this new filter he was surprised at how his questions and comments changed. He found himself asking more clarifying questions, but somehow, this time, they didn't put Iris on edge. Instead, she opened up and became more comfortable as the conversation went on.

By the end of the call, Ethan had a much better handle on where things stood at 10K as a whole. He had even been able to talk over some of the areas he felt might be causing confusion between departments. Feeling more relaxed than he had in days, Ethan realized the pieces of the puzzle were forming in his mind again. That central thread for a new strategy was coming together. "All this is looking great," he said at last to Iris.

At her skeptical look, Ethan paused and reassured her. "I know we're not where we thought we were going to be. But I'm starting to see some of the disconnects. I don't want you to sweat over your client meetings next week. We are all going to get on the same page before those calls." He saw relief wash over Iris's face.

"Thanks, Ethan. This has been really helpful," she said. "I just didn't want to promise the client anything, knowing we might not be able to deliver. I've been worried about this for a while."

After Ethan closed out the meeting, he turned to look out his window. The mountain and sky view seemed endless. He couldn't wait to get home, even with a vista like this. The more he worked through 10K's problems, the more he understood the sign in the lobby. At first, he'd thought that his trust issue was between him and the staff. They hadn't trusted him enough to tell him about delays before things exploded. Then he had realized the problem went deeper, when it became clear that Dom didn't trust Jenna's job performance. And now Iris had added to that the possibility that the client might lose trust in 10K.

Ethan thought about what Amirah had said. A lack of trust is your single greatest expense. He could see it at 10K. The skepticism, the suspicion, the stress. He saw good people, qualified people who had every reason to be totally confident, who ought to be full of great ideas and sure of what they were doing . . . pulling back. These things hadn't shown themselves when business was clipping along without incident. Now, when there was stress, the weaknesses were revealed.

Ethan saw it all much more clearly now. His management team was unsure of how their work fit into the bigger picture. They were afraid of making mistakes, afraid of not getting credit for their ideas, afraid of not being taken seriously or listened to or appreciated. Covering their tracks, waiting for instruction, hesitating to act. Ethan saw cliques and turf wars, the selfishness and the breakdown of communication. He thought about the four stages Sunny had described to him that morning. His "communication" problem was really a lack of clarity.

He saw how people at The Grove rose to the occasion and gave their best, day in and day out. It wasn't just that they were *told* to connect with the guests, or *go the extra mile* in the restaurant, or *maintain stellar performance* in their slope safety teams. They did all those things and a thousand more because they felt safe and empowered to do so.

Ethan hoped he'd be able to accomplish the same kind of culture at 10K. The call with Iris made him think it just might be possible. Sunny was right about building trust. In just one conversation, Ethan could see how his new approach had instantly put Iris at ease. Even after he had upset her in their last meeting, his questions this time had the opposite effect. It had been the most collaborative conversation he'd had in months.

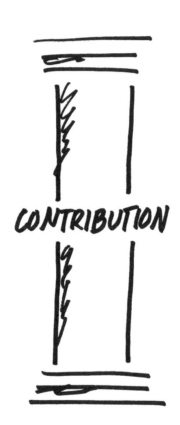

CONTRIBUTION

17
WHAT MATTERS

ON HIS WAY DOWN to grab a light breakfast the next morning, Ethan ran into Naomi, the director of community, who had arranged the big dinner a few nights ago for the Brain Trust—he wouldn't be forgetting that glorious lasagna any time soon.

"Mr. Parker! How are you doing today? I hope your recovery is going well?"

Ethan smiled. "I feel like I've turned the corner on pain, and to be honest, I'm starting to feel like the whole injury was a blessing in disguise. I'm anxious to get home, but it has been fascinating to learn about all the cultural practices and values at The Grove."

Naomi's face lit up. "To be honest, I can't imagine working anywhere else now. And it's not just the camaraderie and support—I've never worked on a more effective team. Everyone who works here, from the ski shop to the executive suite, consistently gets spectacular results. I spent so much time in my former jobs doing performance interventions, but here I barely do any."

Ethan was impressed. He barely ever did performance interventions at 10K, but clearly his approach had led to very different results. "That sounds too good to be true," he said. "Mind sharing your secrets?" Ordinarily he'd never be so bold in asking about another organization's corporate strategy, but everyone at The Grove had made it evident that they were not only willing but enthusiastic about sharing their unique methods and approaches. Naomi was no exception, and as they waited for the elevator, she eagerly dove into her answers.

"One of our eight guiding pillars is **CONTRIBUTION**," she began. "We encourage everyone to be thinking about what they can contribute, rather than what they can get. We also have an excellent compensation and benefits structure, so they are safe knowing that their needs and families are taken care of. Focusing on what they can give necessitates action, and action is what leads to results."

"Isn't that every manager's dream?" Ethan asked. "I'll channel Sunny for a moment—How do you do it?"

Naomi was well practiced at answering that particular question. "There are two important pieces of the puzzle, I think. The first is really a mind-set more than a skill. Imagine each action you made like a stone cast into a big pond. Its ripples radiate out in all directions—going everywhere, touching everything, and affecting everyone. Part of my job is to help our people shift from thinking about the stone to thinking about the ripple."

Ethan nodded, thoughtfully. *To shift from thinking about the stone to thinking about the ripple.* He really liked that image.

"The other piece is concrete and practical, and it's going to sound overly simplistic," she warned. "There is one skill that I'm an absolute fanatic about, and I train every Grove employee in it. It drives cold, hard results better than anything I've ever seen. We train people to ask themselves: 'What's your single priority today?'"

Could it really be that simple? Ethan wondered.

"Of course, you might have a whole list of things that need to get done today," Naomi said as they walked toward the café. "Everyone does. That's fine. A few of those might even be really important, but to make the most effective use of your day—which means the most effective use of yourself—you need to have a single, top-of-mind priority. It's the action through which you can make the biggest difference today. We call it a Difference-Making Action, or DMA for short."

Ethan ordered his coffee and a gingerbread muffin then turned back to Naomi to hear more. This DMA idea was intriguing.

"The staff at The Grove starts each day with the question, What's my top priority today? Some of them even identify it the night before, so in the morning there is no hesitation. What we look for is action that doesn't just produce but also *contributes*. Action that's *meaningful*. Meaningful action tends to produce healthy urgency and momentum." Naomi continued: "It is amazing how often people waste time doing good activities while avoiding taking action on the most important ones. Just imagine what could happen in an organization if everyone started their day by acting on the most important task first." She chuckled then said, "It's actually an old parenting trick. Give your kid one key task to get done today. Not two, not three. Just one. Sure, they will do more than one thing. But the key is to focus on *one* first."

Ethan thanked Naomi for the chat, and she headed to her office. He wasn't sure if it was the strong coffee or the enlightening conversation, but Ethan felt a rush of energy. Both Naomi and Sunny had emphasized the necessity of identifying a single priority. When was the last time he thought about just one priority? It seemed like every day at 10K was a waterfall of to-dos, emails, meetings, and fires to put out.

Ethan thought about what his number-one priority today might be, mentally reviewing his conversations with Jenna, Dom, and Iris. What was the most critical and impactful thing he could do, right now, from here at The Grove? The May 1 deadline was the crucial issue right now, and earlier, Iris had made the very good point that they would have to face that situation as early as next week on status update calls.

A smile tugged at the corner of his mouth. He knew exactly what today's priority was, and he should have time to put the gears in motion before his call with Zach, 10K's director of software, later that afternoon.

A few hours later, Ethan returned to his room and sat down to his check in with the final member of 10K's leadership team. Zach was a certifiable genius, and he could have had his pick of jobs in Silicon Valley or New York. But Minneapolis was his home, and he was more interested in the chance to build something truly innovative than in prestige. Ethan had jumped at the chance to bring Zach on board, and he had never regretted the decision. As smart as he was, though, Zach was not much of a people person. He tended to delegate much of the actual management of his division to his direct reports, while keeping his own focus on the code. Nevertheless, it was Zach's vision for the program they were building that led the way for all of their software development.

Ethan signed on to the call, but Zach was not there yet. A minute went by, then two, then three more. At 3:06 Zach's screen blinked into view. Fiddling with his camera, Zach mumbled a polite greeting and vague apology for being late. When he finally sat back into his chair, he looked at everything in his office other than the computer screen. After a few questions about the status of Zach's division, Ethan could tell something was wrong. Zach was answering, but it was like pulling teeth. Ethan was glad this conversation had come later in the week! Last week, he would probably have gotten defensive and frustrated, or he might have tried to crack a joke—the wrong approach, he now understood.

Today, he deployed another tactic. "Zach, can we stop for a minute? It'd be great to just check in with you."

"Sure, that's fine with me," said Zach with some skepticism.

"So, um," Ethan started cautiously. "I know we have all been nose to the grindstone even before last week, but I just wanted to see how you are doing." Zach tended to keep to himself, and Ethan realized he didn't really know what was going on in Zach's life.

"*Doing?*" Zach's usually flat business façade cracked as his eyes widened, staring straight at the screen now. "Ethan, my team is working as hard as they can, putting in extra hours to cover for Brady, after the accident, and my wife is due any day now. I'm hardly sleeping at all. I'm fighting an uphill battle at work and at home—I'm doing what you hired me to do, Ethan. I'm doing my best."

Of course, Ethan felt like he'd been hit by a train. Zach was about to be a new father too. How had he forgotten that? He noticed the dark bags under Zach's eyes, the signs of strain on his face. And when Brady had gotten hurt, a car accident? Yes, he remembered now, a hurried chat over lunch. Ethan had simply asked Zack to find a way like he always did. How had he become so out of touch with his team? *His* people? He'd been so focused on the beautiful vision and strategy. With his eyes on the horizon, he'd somehow forgotten that they still had to build the road to it—together.

Ethan put his hands to his temples, feeling horrible. "Zach, I am so sorry. I can't believe I have been so out of touch. You must be under a huge amount of strain. How is your wife doing?" It was an unpleasant thought, but Ethan suddenly wondered if his "leadership" problem might actually be a compassion issue.

Zach leaned forward and rested his elbows on his desk, looking deflated after his outburst. "She's great, really, we're both just tired. Though of course nothing like it's going to be once the baby comes, so I'm told."

Ethan laughed. He and Maya were in for a few years of sleepless nights as well. Sunny's advice about asking himself whether or not he was being compassionate echoed in his mind. "Zach, let me run something by you. With one programmer on leave, and you about to become a father, would it help to bring on a few more folks for your department? Could you train some new programmers if we hired folks with the right skill set?"

"Well, I guess so . . . ," Zach said slowly.

Ethan's excitement got the better of him, as his ideas rushed out. "I've been meaning to implement a formal paternity leave for a while now. There's no time like the present, right? If you could onboard two or even three new people, that might give you the flexibility to take some real time off." He was feeling more confident by the second. He'd always had the best of intentions for his staff, but it was becoming increasingly clear that his actions hadn't lived up to those intentions.

Zach stared directly at the screen, eyebrows raised. It probably seemed like this idea had come out of left field, but Ethan had been thinking about all the support structures he had seen at The Grove: a CEO helping a member of the kitchen staff find housing; Naomi planning a whole dinner for Ethan and his friends; the dedicated hours of training and development; asking what the organization could do for the employees instead of the other way round. Ethan felt humbled; he didn't have nearly the same level of staff support infrastructure at 10K, but this felt like the right thing to do, and maybe it would be a good start.

Zach was flabbergasted, not sure how to respond. "Well . . . I," he stammered, "that would be awesome, Ethan, you would do that? I mean, do we have the budget for it? And things are so behind—do you really think taking time off would be a good call right now?"

"Absolutely, Zach. We may have hit a rough patch, but the budget, at least for now, is solid. The company's important, but you are too. And I have faith in your team. I promise, going forward, I won't let important things like this fall off my radar again."

18
FULL CIRCLE

IT WAS 9:30 BY THE TIME Ethan finished writing out his notes in the Great Room. He'd never have thought that a ski accident would be the best thing ever to happen to him and to 10K—yet here he was, hundreds of miles from home, running his business more effectively than he had in months. Not only had his conversations with Sunny and other Grove employees taught him a new way of thinking, his meetings with the 10K leadership team had already started to have an impact. And his final conversation with Sunny that evening had clicked in a way that felt real. Ethan was ready to go home.

Just before returning his borrowed copy of *Prince Caspian*, Ethan remembered to remove the napkin drawing of the 8 Pillars, which he now placed into his notebook. Scanning the eight C's—clarity, connection, contribution, compassion, competency, character, commitment, and consistency—he mentally matched the pillars with conversations he'd had over the course of the week. Commitment and consistency were left, ideas he might have connected with trust even before he arrived at The Grove.

But the two pillars reminded him of his conversation with his buddy Tripper about their early ski trips. No matter what, Ethan had always found a way to make their trips happen.

As a college student, J.J. had never skied before, and didn't have much money for ski lessons, so Ethan had taught him the basics. When they were all starting out with no money to their names, Ethan found hostels and scoured the country for deals and affordable lift passes. Then the demands of entrepreneurship increased, and it had seemed like the trips were going to fade in the face of expanded responsibilities and scheduling challenges. But Ethan always found a way. It was that refusal to give up that had held the Brain Trust together all these years. Ethan's relationships with his friends were a rock in his life that was every bit as strong as his relationship with Maya. In fact, he realized, it was the trust in those relationships that had made Ethan feel safe enough to acknowledge that he himself bore a lot of the responsibility for what had happened at 10K.

He looked up just in time to see Chef Lou, still in his white coat, walking out of the restaurant carrying two small bowls. Ethan's hopeful wave was rewarded as Lou sauntered over and sat down next to him.

"I thought I'd bring you the last of the ginger snaps and ice cream myself," he said, offering one of the bowls to Ethan. "Mind if I join you?"

"Please do," said Ethan with gratitude, immediately digging in. The dessert was just as good as the first time around, and the ginger snaps had developed that satisfying crunch that always took a few days.

"So, you learning anything useful from our little establishment?" Lou asked. He'd been at the meeting in the Treehouse, so he knew all about Ethan's crash course in trust.

"I really am, Lou. And it's already changing the way I interact with my staff back home. I was just thinking about the commitment pillar, actually. I haven't talked about it explicitly with anyone yet. If you are willing, I'd love to hear a little more about that one."

Lou leaned back thoughtfully, after taking a bite of his own bowl of ice cream. "You know, I came out here from New York City. A few of us have actually. The Manhattan restaurant scene is a tough one—brutal, I'd go so far as to say—and I was burned out. Being a chef is a challenging career in the best of cases; you're always on your feet, carrying fifty pound bags of flour around on your shoulders; dealing with the heat of the ovens; and you have to move fast, since every night is a roller coaster. And don't get me started on industry politics." He shook his head, giving Ethan a frank stare. "I needed a change."

"So what made up your mind?" asked Ethan. "Why here?"

"I wasn't sure about anything initially, to tell you the truth," the chef said. "I didn't know much about Colorado, and I hadn't ever been skiing before in my life. But in the culinary world it's normal to head off to a resort in some remote place you've never been to, so I took a chance."

Things had clearly worked out for him. "What made you want to stay?"

"It's funny you asked me about **COMMITMENT**," Lou said, "because that's what it was. At first, coming out to a state like Colorado, I was a little apprehensive. As a Black man from Brooklyn, I wasn't sure what kind of connection I'd be able to make out here." He pointed out that despite the restaurant industry's extensive diversity, it was concentrated at the bottom. "As you climb the ranks," he explained, "it becomes even more predominantly male, and predominantly white. So for all the diversity of the line cooks and the busboys and the waitstaff, it's still a culture that has a long way to go in terms of creating a welcoming space where everyone's voice can be heard and where folks are valued for who they are. And it's that commitment pillar that makes all the difference. You can't hire a 'diverse' staff and think you are done. You can't do a one-day training and expect it to fix decades of inequality."

What Lou was saying about longer-term efforts made sense logically, but Ethan wasn't sure what else you could be committed to, once you'd already committed to greater equity. Tentatively, he asked, "What does that commitment look like? I guess I'll channel Sunny again and ask you her favorite question: How?"

Lou smiled warmly as he answered: "I think the real difference in what we do here is the focus on action. The whole 8 Pillar model is rooted in immediate, everyday actions. If you haven't identified a way to take action, you haven't gone deep enough. And that's what's missing in so much diversity and inclusion work: Action. Since action is The Grove's default setting, all the work around equity ends up being much more meaningful. It has a real impact."

Ethan felt a twinge of discomfort. Lou's description of diversity in action made 10K's efforts seem decidedly lackluster. "I'm ashamed to admit it, but I feel like I could be doing a much better job at this myself. I don't even see where to start sometimes. This week has been a gift, and I want to go back home and make some real changes."

"The most valuable lesson, I think, is to recognize that things still aren't perfect," Lou responded. As he spoke, Ethan marveled again at the openness and candor with which The Grove's employees were consistently willing to share. "People make mistakes—Sunny makes mistakes. But the critical difference is that when Sunny makes a mistake, she listens, and she listens from a place of humility. She recognizes that she and everyone else still have a long way to go. But we're all in the soup together here. No one is throwing darts from the sidelines."

"You know, you can't always say that about a place," mused Ethan. "So often it seems like everyone's got an answer, but no one is asking the questions. And I think I have to face up to the fact that I've been just as guilty of that." He thought with some chagrin about the mind-mapping board in his office, which he had done entirely by himself. He had been proud of that, but now he felt embarrassed. It really should have been a team effort.

Lou had finished his own dessert but didn't seem in a hurry to go anywhere. "It really does start with listening," he said. "Learning to listen is important to all of us here; it's part of the very fabric of the lodge's culture. Equipping all employees with the skills to meaningfully engage with all perspectives, especially those different from their own, is one of our highest priorities here. But most importantly, Sunny is learning to lead alongside us, rather than assuming she knows more than anyone on the team because of her leadership position.

"Let me tell you a story," Lou said, settling into his chair. "A few years after I graduated, one of my classmates from the Culinary Institute ended up working as the sous chef for a year at an elite hotel restaurant. She had been the top of our class, and everyone knew her star was rising. Chef after chef quit, and every time, for a month or two, the board made her the interim chef, just until they hired a replacement. When she finally went to them and asked to take the position permanently, since she'd decisively proven herself, they turned her down flat. They didn't give a real reason, but all the chefs they hired were men."

Lou paused, then said: "I guess in order to really see, you've got to be looking."

Ethan nodded, taking it all in and wondering how he could take action in a meaningful way.

"All that is to say," Lou continued, "making the workplace an equitable place is the longest game there is, and that's something that takes unwavering dedication and commitment. You've got to build accountability into the system so it's present for everyone, every day. You've got to work on it intentionally, and you can't walk away when it gets uncomfortable. Sunny Bonaventure really understands what commitment means, and that's why I've stayed."

Ethan thought about all the moments of recognition he'd had over the past week, moments where he saw trust at work in his own life: the Brain Trust's dedication to each other; his relationship with Maya. It was true that in the most trusting relationships in his life, there was a rock-solid current of commitment behind everything.

Lou reached for his bowl, and sat forward on the edge of the armchair. He seemed about to get up, and Ethan followed suit, recognizing that the conversation was coming to a close. But Lou shared one more thought before heading back to the restaurant.

"You see, one of the major issues with all those diverse kitchens where I got my start, was that they had a lot of diversity, but absolutely no trust. Diversity without trust actually makes problems worse. When people who have different life experiences are expected to work alongside each other, conflict will increase if there is a lack of trust and a minimal ability to build shared understanding. In a way, what I've realized here is that more than anything, trust is the crux. Diversity alone will never work without it. You need diversity, equity, and trust. Inclusion might be the goal, but you'll never get inclusion without trust."

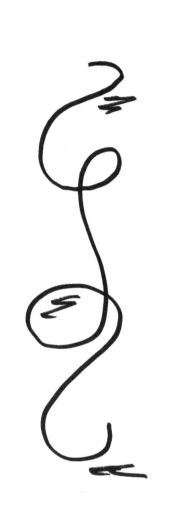

19
THE MAIN THREAD

THURSDAY MORNING Ethan sat in the Reading Room, waiting for a last quick meeting with Sunny. He was filled with relief and anticipation; the surgeon had cleared him to fly home as early as tomorrow. This week at The Grove had been an amazing experience, but Ethan couldn't wait to get back to Maya and 10K. He booked a 10:00 AM flight, which would get him to Minneapolis just in time to gather the team for a 3:00 meeting. Ethan had a few surprises for them, and he wanted to wrap up the week on a positive note.

He was just sending off an email with the good news and his meeting request when a soft chime announced the elevator's arrival. Sunny gave a little wave and called out a "Good morning!" as she made her way across the room. Ethan wanted to thank her for taking such a special interest in his work, his injury, and his life.

"Thanks for meeting with me," he said. "I just saw the doc again."

"And?"

"She gave me the all-clear to fly. I've got a flight booked for tomorrow morning. I'm on my way home!" Ethan grinned.

"I'm so glad!" Sunny exclaimed. "I hope you've enjoyed your week here and gotten plenty of rest! And maybe even a little inspiration?"

Sunny sat down across from Ethan and set a small weekend bag down at her feet. "More than a little," he said with all the sincerity he could muster. "I can't thank you enough, Sunny, truly."

She tilted her head and said, "Our pleasure."

"When I got here on Thursday, I was a complete mess," Ethan said. "I felt like my company was probably toast, and I hadn't seen it coming at all." He still couldn't believe how out of touch he'd become.

Sunny nodded, her expression both supportive and sympathetic. "It's tough to be the Lone Ranger, Ethan. In fact, it's almost impossible. That's why building trust is so important."

It had been important for Ethan to hear Sunny's experience as a leader. He knew she'd understand his regret. "I let them down, Sunny. I'm the CEO, the head of the company. Heck, I *founded* it—my team should have been able to trust me to lead them in the right direction and head this stuff off before it happened . . . ," he trailed off, thinking of all the revelations that had surfaced over the last few days. "I've learned so much, and I am deeply grateful to you. I was completely oblivious. Who knows how long I would have gone on the same way, never fixing the problem, letting things get worse and worse?"

"That's just it though, isn't it?" Sunny said. "No one realizes they have a trust problem. And that's the whole problem."

She was right of course. Ethan laughed and raised a hand to his face. It really wasn't rocket science, was it? "I didn't realize I had a problem," he said. "My problem . . . was that I didn't know I had a problem!" After that disastrous meeting with his team last week, Ethan had been in denial. Even when he'd asked himself why his team didn't trust him, back in the empty conference room in Minneapolis, he hadn't realized he had a trust problem. At least, not in the way he now understood trust, thanks to his week at The Grove.

Sunny looked him square in the eye. "That's the hardest thing about leading, Ethan, having to see what's hardest to see. The Lone Ranger can't look all ways at once, but with a team that trusts their leader to accept honest feedback, no matter what it is? That leader will hear about problems the instant they arise. That's why we have the sign in the lobby. People trust what they are empowered to be a real part of, where they feel that they are recognized and valued both as employees and as human beings. That will manifest in everything they do."

Ethan got it. He knew things would be different—his entire perspective had shifted. "I think I understand what you were saying the other day. It's not enough to be a trustworthy person—you have to build a trustworthy business. Not in the sense of not cheating people, that's obvious, but one where the fabric of the whole organization, from the business model to employee relationships, is based on real trust." He looked around the beautiful Reading Room. "Like you've done here."

The elevator chimed softly again, and Milo peeked into the room. "Mom? The truck's warmed up and ready when you are. Good to see you again, Mr. Parker!" He waved and popped back into the elevator before the doors closed. Sunny gestured to the bag at her feet and explained that she and Milo were taking off for the weekend, to visit family in Montana.

Rising to his feet, gathering up the crutches under his left arm, Ethan shook Sunny's hand. "Thanks. For the week. Just thanks . . . for everything. And do thank Milo again for saving my knee! You've raised a good son."

Sunny Bonaventure beamed. "You're welcome, Ethan Parker."

20
THE WAY FORWARD

THE CAB PULLED UP TO THE CURB in front of the 10K offices and Ethan opened the door in excitement. From the airport, he'd made a quick stop at home to say hello to Maya and drop his gear off. He would be right on time for the 3:00 meeting. As the cab pulled away, Ethan leaned on his crutches and looked up at the office building for a moment. He marveled at how much had happened since he was last here. Dejected, panicked, guilty—and now here he was, inspired and hopeful. He had faith everything he learned during his stay at The Grove worked because he had already started to implement it.

Sunny was right—trust could be built in a moment. He'd even had one final conversation about trust with Eddie, The Grove's elderly driver who had taken him to the airport that morning.

"Good to be getting back home?" Eddie had asked, breaking Ethan's train of thought.

"Sorry?"

"I was just saying," Eddie repeated, "it's always good to get back home again."

"That it is. Though I have to say, I've had quite the week at The Grove."

"No place like it," Eddie said. "I see a lot of happy guests here. I've been working for the Bonaventures for forty years now. Good people. The best." They drove on in companionable silence for a few minutes before Eddie spoke up again. "It must be good to be getting home, though. Telling your wife, 'I love you' on the phone is good, but not the same as being there. You have to fill up that cup of appreciation and love every day. You want that cup to runneth over, know what I mean?"

Ethan agreed, already looking forward to giving Maya the biggest bear hug ever as soon as he got home.

"You can't just say something like that once and decide, 'Hey, I'm done.' You don't build a happy marriage on the big gesture once a year, you build it on the little things you say and do every day," Eddie said, sounding as if he knew a thing or two about a happy marriage.

Ethan thought about how important it was to him to make sure to kiss Maya every time he left the house for work. About how, every night before they went to sleep, he told her that he loved her. And how, in the saying of it, he realized all over again how much he really meant it.

Eddie's self-assured tone spoke from the accumulated wisdom of a lifetime, and Ethan was happy to listen to the older man's calming voice as they drove through the wintery Colorado land-scape. "If you want people to trust your business, you have to have **CONSISTENCY**," Eddie said. "Being committed when things are looking good, that just isn't commitment. Character once in a while is no character at all."

It's true, Ethan thought. *You don't usually get one big chance to earn someone's trust. You get a thousand little chances. And they all count.* Eddie echoed his own thoughts. "It's the little things that matter. They add up to big things."

And now here Ethan was, about to meet his team in person, and he couldn't wait to keep doing more of those little things. He took the elevator up to the fifth floor and headed straight to the conference room, where the team was already waiting for him. After a round of greetings and concerned questions about his knee, he settled at the front of the room. He'd been planning what he wanted to say for hours. He opened the meeting with an apology.

"I have a confession to make," Ethan said. "Over the past year I've made a lot of assumptions, many of them incorrect. I failed to set clear expectations and priorities, and I haven't established an environment where people can do their best work—where *you* can do your best work. As big as 10K has grown, I am still not used to sharing my thought process. And as a result, I've dropped the ball on asking for details on processes from you all as well. I just assumed you were getting it done." Ethan paused. This was challenging to admit, but he thought about the successful moments he'd already had with his team and kept going.

"I think every division at 10K has become isolated, feeling like they can share only the bare minimum of information with others, and that falls on me. I haven't done my best to build a culture that encourages trust. I was too focused on the big picture, and I neglected to facilitate communication and collaboration. Honestly, it's no wonder we weren't reaching our targets."

Ethan looked around to take stock. The feeling in the room was completely different than it had been the week before. "Last Thursday, I asked you all what the chances were of hitting our deadline. You did your best to answer—but I was asking the wrong question. The truth is, if I'm going to be fully honest about it, we've already missed it."

Iris shifted in her chair, and the team glanced around at each other, clearly uncomfortable. Ethan looked down at the table for a moment, and then looked up with a confident smile. "I have an announcement to make today," he continued. "Yesterday afternoon I called the CEOs of the five biggest client stakeholders in our investor consortium. I explained the scenario to them, and that May 1 is not a realistic timeframe for us anymore. I'll be frank, some were more understanding than others. But ultimately, I was able to get everyone on our side. I committed to deliver *something* by that date, something substantial enough to show our quality of work and our dedication. I also promised to establish a new timeline, with a real deadline by which we can positively deliver."

Zach was smiling openly, surprised and relieved. Iris looked like a huge weight had been lifted from her shoulders. Jenna gave Ethan a nod of approval, and Dom sat at the other end of the room, leaning back in his chair, a look of quiet satisfaction across his face.

Ethan could tell from their reactions that he was on the right track. Sunny had been right—about everything. With just a few small changes, he could already tell that trust was returning to 10K, bit by bit. Hitting the new preliminary deadline would not be sufficient to set the trust dial back to ground level. To fully regain the consortium's trust, they would need to meet every commitment beyond that, on time, no matter what. They would have to win, win, and win. But Ethan wasn't worried. He had every faith they could do it.

"I know my choice not to cancel my ski weekend in Colorado in the midst of this crisis was probably an irresponsible one, and I am very sorry for the distress it may have caused," he told the team. "However, getting stuck there ended up being the most important learning experience of my life. I learned so much from the people I met, and I am so excited to share everything with you all. I want to be very clear: 10K is still in a crisis. If we miss the next deadline, it will be game over. But one of the things I've learned is a method for tackling a crisis."

Ethan shared the two crisis response questions Sunny had explained, the clarity and simplicity of the two questions: What can I control? And what should I do right now? The questions opened the floodgates, and the team talked enthusiastically about what they could do. Information was flowing, and ideas were pouring out of everyone in the room.

This is just the beginning, Ethan thought.

That evening, Ethan sat on his own couch, in front of his own fire, telling Maya all about The Grove. There was no breathtaking vista of mountaintops outside his window, but he was home. Even so, The Grove had one final lesson for him. As Ethan told Maya all about Sunny and Milo, the Reading Room, Lou, Naomi, and the others, he saw trust in yet another new light.

He'd been so focused on what he could learn from Sunny about saving his business that he hadn't thought about everywhere else trust might show up in his life. As he told Maya about his strange, wonderful week, he realized that at every turn, the important insights he'd made had been, first and foremost, about Maya or the Brain Trust. Thinking about the connection he had with the Brain Trust was how he'd first made the link from the connection pillar to trust. It was Sunny's reference to his habit of telling Maya he loved her every day that had helped him to wake up to the power of clarity and consistency. He recognized that commitment was the bedrock beneath everything. And most of all, it was the parenting adventure he and Maya were about to begin that had inspired him to hire additional programmers for Zach, taking concrete steps to show compassion for his colleagues.

Trust wasn't just going to help 10K, it was going to help his friendships, his marriage, his whole life. *Trust really is everywhere*, Ethan thought. Trust is everything.

Epilogue
RETURN

TEN MONTHS LATER, THE AIR had begun to take on the familiar late autumn chill. Ethan gave Maya a hug as they waited at the carousel for their bags at the Denver airport. Her mother was taking care of their baby boy, Henry. He was both the most wonderful and the most chaotic thing ever to happen to Ethan's life, and Ethan marveled at how much he already missed Henry, not even three hours later. But Ethan and Maya were on their way to The Grove for a long weekend. Maya had successfully defended her dissertation, and they were taking the weekend to celebrate. He couldn't wait for her to see the mountain and to meet everyone at The Grove. And he wanted to go back to the place that had given him the inspiration he needed to lead his team to a successful completion of 10K's major projects.

The plan Ethan and the team had worked out when he returned from Colorado had succeeded beyond his wildest dreams. The consortium had rallied after getting the updated status report, and they worked with 10K to adjust timelines. Ethan had used the methods and mind-sets he'd learned at The Grove to guide him the whole way. 10K now had thriving mastermind groups and a small but growing library. He started asking how 10K could do more for its staff, and retention had skyrocketed—a crucial factor as they pushed to meet their new deadlines.

Some of Sunny's 8 Pillars, as it turned out, had been in worse shape than others. There were some that just needed shoring up. Competency, for example, and contribution were in pretty good shape. Others, such as connection and consistency, needed to be practically rebuilt from scratch, stone by stone. Ethan had the entire organization do the Trust Shield exercise he had learned from J.J., and new friendships had spring up all over the company. He trained his whole team to ask "How?" and once they understood the method, they'd all had a good laugh about Ethan's first stumbling attempts.

It had not been smooth sailing the entire way—that's for sure—but they'd made it through. The team at 10K Solutions met their deadlines and their work was well on its way to being considered the new industry standard. Ethan still had insecurities, but he understood himself and his colleagues much better after all the trust building he and his colleagues had done since that fateful ski accident. He owed Sunny a debt of gratitude.

And now here they were, and the mountain awaited Ethan and Maya.

"Good afternoon, Mr. Parker!" Eddie greeted him. "Looking good without those crutches! And this must be Mrs. Parker! It's so nice to meet you." He lead Ethan and Maya toward the waiting car. "Welcome back to Colorado," he said as the airport doors slid open.

Ethan was carrying with him a special gift for Sunny, a piece of artwork of sorts. It was the cocktail napkin illustrating the 8 Pillars that she had drawn out for him in the Reading Room ten months earlier, matted and framed. A copy hung on his own office wall, directly across from his desk, where he could see it every day.

consistency
clarity
compassion
character
contribution
competency
connection
commitment

THE
APPLICATION

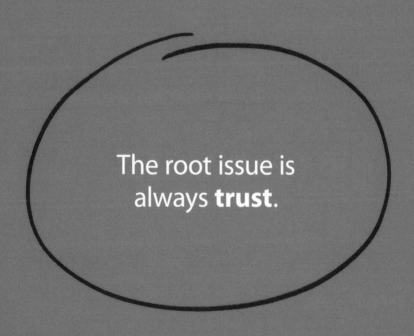

The root issue is
always **trust**.

21
THE CASE FOR TRUST

JUST LIKE ETHAN PARKER'S TEAM at 10K, the number one question everyone is asking about you is, "Can I trust you?" Many people think we follow and buy from people we like, but that is only partly true. I have a friend who I like hanging out with, but I would not go into business with him in a million years because I don't trust him. Everyone wants to be liked. But trust is much more valuable, and if you build trust genuinely, your likeability will almost always go up as well.

Everything of value is built on trust. At the core, problems are never about leadership, communication, sales, marketing, or even finances. The research and the work we do in companies and governments around the world reveals that the main problem is always rooted in some type of trust issue. A leader is followed because he or she is trusted. Salespeople close sales because of trust. The only way to amplify a marketing message is to increase the audience's trust in the message. When teams trust each other, they are willing to share ideas and innovation, and therefore creativity goes up. Even diversity can pit people against each other unless there is a culture of trust. A wide range of organizational and leadership issues can be solved using one or more of the 8 Pillars of Trust—the ones Sunny sketched out for Ethan when they first met in the Reading Room at The Grove.

Trust will always increase effectiveness and create lasting results in your organization. Remember:

🍸 A lack of trust is your biggest expense.

🍸 The number one question everyone wants to know the answer to is "Can I trust you?"

🍸 The 8 Pillars of Trust are the foundation for effective leadership and cultures where people can perform at their best.

🍸 Everything of value is built on trust.

The 8 Pillars of Trust are woven throughout *Trusted Leader*. Which one did you identify with the most? Which one represents an area in which you'd like to improve?

The Research

In working with businesses and organizations large and small, I consistently observe one fundamental truth at the root all of their failures and successes, struggles and solutions: *Trust affects everything.*

This truth first became apparent during my graduate work in organizational leadership. I took a deep dive into existing research on what traits characterized the most successful leaders and organizations. The conclusion of that research has been borne out again and again, not only in my consulting work but also in all of our continuing research and our annual global trust study, *The Trust Outlook.*

When trust increases, so does output, morale, retention, innovation, loyalty, and productivity. When trust decreases, costs, problems, attrition, stress, and time-to-market all increase. No matter your goals, challenges, or circumstances, authentic long-term success cannot be achieved until a significant level of trust is established. Remember when Ethan Parker first arrived at The Grove? That sign at the entrance is true: *Trust is everything.*

Trust is your single most valuable asset.

From personal relationships to financial institutions, everything of value is built on trust. Here are a few findings from our annual research publication, *The Trust Outlook*:

- The number one reason people give for wanting to work for an organization is trusted leadership. It is rated higher than a raise, good benefits, more autonomy, or a fun work environment.

- Most millennials would take a pay cut if they could trust their leadership.

- More than twelve million Americans have invested $100,000 or more based purely on trusting someone else.

- 85 percent say a high-trust environment helps them perform at their best.

- When employees trust senior leadership, they offer more ideas and solutions, are better team players, and are significantly more loyal.

- In a climate of trust, people are more willing to work together, be creative, share information, and stay motivated and productive. They demonstrate loyalty and a commitment to the team and are willing to go the extra mile to ensure success. Every aspect of the business becomes more profitable.

With greater trust, customers will pay more, tell others, and return again and again. With suppliers whom we trust, one call is enough. Delivery time and costs decrease because there is less need for double-checking, paperwork, and follow-up.

Create a bedrock of trust and *everything* changes. Trust is your greatest competitive advantage!

A lack of trust is your biggest expense.

Trust is not only your business's most precious resource but also one of its most fragile. Just as increased trust can accelerate any business, organization, or relationship, so can mistrust erode, weaken, and ultimately destroy it.

Scan any company's balance sheet, and you won't see any column with the heading of "Trust." It's not something we typically think of as having an economic value per se. But scratch the surface of all those numbers, take a hard look at what is reflected in the data, and you find trust—or lack of trust—everywhere you look.

A focus on trust is necessary at every level, especially at the level of governance. Losing trust is your biggest risk as a board. Any board's key job is maintaining and increasing trust. From cyber sabotage, to moral failures, to leadership—your biggest risk is losing trust. And it's not just the obvious things, such as litigation, fraud, or plummeting sales due to loss of trust in the marketplace. Lack of trust also shows up in the day-to-day costs of doing business. When trust is absent, skepticism and suspicion erode relationships. This slows down the flow of ideas and the ability to solve problems. Everything takes longer and work conditions become stressful and unhealthy.

I cover the case for trust more extensively in my 2012 book *The Trust Edge*, but consider the example here that Amirah, The Grove's director of finance, shares with Ethan: Mr. Olson's fruit and vegetable stand, which is a true story from my own child-hood in rural Minnesota. The expense of staffing the fruit and veggie stand would have started with paying the employee, but the costs wouldn't have ended there. Think of all the cascading liabilities of having employees in the first place: insurance, risk of on-the-job injury, maintaining an employment lawyer. Even if Mr. Olson or his family had staffed the stand, that would have taken up most of their precious hours, necessitated setting up and breaking down every day, and limited the hours people could shop. Cost would pile up on top of cost. And in addition to saving money, the trusting relationship Mr. Olson had with the community saved the day when his barn caught fire.

Take another example, this one almost universal: How long does it take to write a text to someone you trust? Zip and you are done! You don't even need to take the time to read it over because you know they will understand, typos and all. Now, how long does it take to write a text to someone you *don't* trust? It can take an eternity because of the second-guessing and fear that you will not be given the benefit of the doubt regarding your text.

Trust is the root cause of every issue, and at the end of the day a lack of trust always costs money, whether that lack is costing time, attrition, stress, duplication of efforts, or productivity at first glance. The fastest way to go out of business is to lose trust.

Trust is your leading indicator.

Businesses use dozens of different key performance indicators (KPIs) to assess their relative health and progress toward their goals. Many KPIs have great validity, in and of themselves. The problem is, many of them don't get at the heart of the matter. For example, one common goal is to increase engagement. However, you don't increase engagement by adding more engagement. The only way to increase engagement is to increase trust. When trust in teams goes up, people feel safe and valued so they are willing to share ideas and praise, which in turn leads to increased innovation and productivity. Higher engagement scores are the natural outcome of a high-trust culture. It starts with trust.

Net Promoter Score (NPS)—developed by Fred Reichheld, Bain & Company, and Satmetrix—is often used as a metric of customer loyalty. NPS is based on how your customers answer the question, "Would you refer us to someone else?" It's an excellent and simple question that gets at trust on a broader scale. The only way to get more referrals is to increase trust. These conclusions are not just opinion; the data backs it up. For example, our 2019 *Trust Outlook* found that nine out of ten people won't refer people they don't trust. This fundamental truth applies even to the sensitive issue of diversity. Harvard political scientist Robert Putnam's important study of diversity based on nearly thirty thousand people across America found that diversity on its own can have a negative effect. However, if trust is established, not only will the negative effects of diversity dissipate but a multitude of benefits will arise. If we believe in the value of diversity but aren't seeing the results we'd like, a good first step is to put more emphasis on trust.

The same principle applies to innovation. If members of a team trust each other, they share ideas. Sharing ideas results in more creativity and innovation. If a team doesn't trust one another, they won't feel safe to share ideas, and both creativity and innovation will take a nosedive.

A lack of trust is the core challenge.

Think about your own company or organization: What are the top two or three issues you are facing right now, or have faced in the past year? What are the greatest challenges to your future per-

CASE for TRUST

KICKSTART

CLARITY

COMPASSION

CHARACTER

COMPETENCY

COMMITMENT

CONNECTION

CONTRIBUTION

CONSISTENCY

NEXT STEPS

formance, growth, and stability in the marketplace? Whatever issues you encounter, even though you and I may have never met, I can tell you one thing about those issues with complete confidence: They are, at their core, an issue of trust.

You may believe you're having a leadership issue, but that is only a symptom. People don't follow leaders they don't trust. Perhaps your sales numbers are not where they should be. It's not a sales issue at the core. You're losing sales because your sales force or your potential customers don't trust you. Or let's say you've been told you need better marketing. That may be so—but the only way to amplify a marketing campaign is to increase trust in the delivery of the message. Trust touches everything.

Success is never fundamentally a leadership issue, or a communication issue, or even a resource issue. Success at its core *always* comes as a benefit of being trusted.

Trust is a learnable skill set.

A trust problem doesn't mean you're not a good person, that you don't mean well, or that you don't have everyone's best interests at heart. You can be all those things. I'm sure you *are* all those things. But trust is not something that flows automatically from your good intentions. Active, conscious work is required to *build* trust. When you don't put forth this effort, or when the trust you've built becomes weakened or compromised, this leads to a problem—often a big problem.

The most exciting insight we've learned about trust in business is not only how pivotal it is, but also how *available* it is. Trust, it turns out, is a core competency that can be learned, practiced, and perfected—often with astonishing results. In the work we've done helping people rebuild faltering trust within their businesses and organizations, we've heard everything from "It tripled our sales" to "It saved my marriage!" I have seen opposition leaders of countries that no one believed would ever come together start to build trust in ways that will likely change the world. I have seen hopeless organizations and leaders prioritize trust and see results they did not believe were possible.

The results are undeniable.

Consider the following results that our clients over the years have attributed to their work with the Trust Edge Leadership Institute:

- ⊤ A $1 billion company increased their market share 10 percent in one year.

- ⊤ A multibillion-dollar company increased their engagement score for the first time in fourteen years.

- ⊤ A medium-sized company eliminated $2.4 million in attrition costs in nine months.

- ⊤ The coach of a college football team took his team from a record of 3–7 to 7–3 in one season.

But ultimately the most profound impact I've witnessed from this work has been personal. It changed my marriage, it changed my personal life, and it changed me. We know trust is critical. We know building or rebuilding trust is possible. Let's look at *how* we can actually build trust.

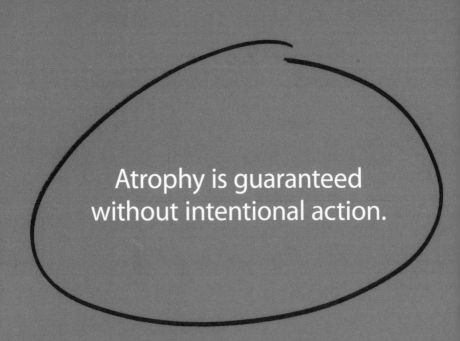

Atrophy is guaranteed
without intentional action.

CASE 4 TRUST

KICKSTART

CLARITY

COMPASSION

CHARACTER

COMPETENCY

COMMITMENT

CONNECTION

CONTRIBUTION

CONSISTENCY

NEXT STEPS

22
KICKSTARTING TRUST

ETHAN DECIDES TO USE Sunny's own strategy of asking "How?" to try and figure out what to do to save 10K Solutions. In answer, she walks him through a four-stage process that you can use to start building trust in your own organization. Going through these stages with intention and focus will form the foundation for trust to take root and then grow in a long-lasting and sustainable way.

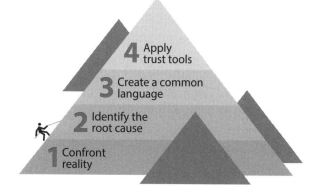

1. Confront Reality

Before Ethan leaves The Grove, he has the final realization that his real problem was that *he didn't know he had a problem.* The first thing leaders or coaches need to do is help their team or client to confront reality. The disastrous meeting that revealed Ethan's problems was a spectacular crash and burn, and you hopefully won't experience such a disastrous precipitating event. Instead, you might start by measuring trust with a tool like our Enterprise Trust Index. Help your people see the real problem. Where have things broken down? Where are things working less than optimally?

2. Identify the Root Cause

Learning the root cause of a breakdown can be painful. If you think you have a leadership problem, think about where, under the radar, trust might have been degrading to *cause* the leadership problem. Dig down to see how trust relates to your key issues. Some people think they have a communication issue. It's actually a trust issue. Or maybe there is plenty of communication, but it's not clear communication.

3. Create a Common Language

Creating a common language makes solving any problem a much faster process. It unifies teams and helps give them the chance to solve the real issue on common ground. The clarity pillar is key to this stage. Identify your issues and use clear and consistent language going forward to talk through your challenges. Use the 8 Pillars of Trust as a foundation for this common language.

4. Apply Trust Tools

Since the root cause is always a trust issue, you need research-based, actionable tools and frameworks that are applicable right now. You've already been introduced to many trust-building tools through the conversations Ethan has with various staff members at The Grove, and the next section elaborates on those and introduces more tools.

The 8 Pillars of Trust

At the heart of my original research, I made two critical findings. The first is that *trust is the single greatest metric for success.* The second is that *there is a way to build or rebuild trust.* As I pondered, "How does one increase trust?" my inquiry led me to discover the eight specific traits the most trusted leaders, brands, and organizations have in common. When even one of these eight traits is weak, trust will predictably be compromised. When all eight traits are present, trust will be strong. Strength in all 8 Pillars of Trust leads to the greatest advantage in business and in life, which I have come to call *The Trust Edge.*

In our story, Ethan encounters the 8 Pillars through Sunny, his friends in the Brain Trust, Sunny's son Milo, and many other employees at The Grove. The Grove might not be a real place, but there are companies all over the world that, knowingly or not, practice the 8 Pillars and have thriving businesses with workplace cultures as vibrant and successful as this imaginary ski lodge. This trust framework was an extremely exciting discovery. It meant that in any case where a business is struggling, places more like 10K Solutions than like The Grove, not only will we find a predictable lack of trust, we will also find concrete, diagnosable reasons for the weakness—and they are fixable!

It is true that in a given situation, some of these traits may be more important than others. If I'm hiring a nanny for my kids, for instance, I'm watching out for *compassion* and *character* more than *clarity*. If you're the surgeon about to operate on my child, I'm not too concerned with your *connection*, but I am keenly interested in your *competency*! By and large, though, all 8 Pillars are relatively coequal, and for the structure of trust to stand—all 8 Pillars need to be present, healthy, and strong.

Like the columns of a building, the pillars hold up the entire edifice. When one or more of the 8 Pillars is weakened, the structure itself is in danger of collapse. In the case of 10K, the company was naturally excelling in some pillars. But other pillars had weakened to the point of total collapse. The strength of the pillars the company did well in couldn't make up for the weakness in all the others. This shows how important it is to diagnose organizational problems and arrive at the necessary remedies. With a breadth of experience coupled with our ongoing research, I believe every organizational and leadership issue can be solved by using this framework. I am not saying it is easy, or that contextualization is not necessary. I am saying that every issue falls under one or more of the 8 Pillars of Trust. For this reason it is valuable to create a common language around trust in organizations that want to enjoy the benefits of a high-trust culture.

Ethan was not able to get a comprehensive master class in the details of every single pillar during his stay at The Grove. But the remainder of this book provides insights and takeaways into each of the 8 Pillars to help drive your own results. There is a description of each pillar, what it looks like when that pillar is weakened, and suggestions on how to strengthen that particular pillar. An in-depth discussion of all 8 Pillars, including more suggestions for how to strengthen them within your own business or organization, can be found in the book *The Trust Edge* or at www.Trust Edge.com.

CLARITY

People trust the clear and mistrust the ambiguous.

23
PILLAR 1: CLARITY

CLARITY IS THE CORNERSTONE of trust. We tend to trust someone when we know where they stand, and when they are clear in their words and actions. The more vague or ambiguous, the more difficult it is to trust someone. This is why, for example, the military places an extreme value on clarity. It is nearly impossible to maintain a reliable chain of command structure unless all those involved trust their superiors—no matter what. And it is difficult to trust someone who is not crystal clear, especially when the stakes are high!

In our story, Sunny Bonaventure particularly valued the pillar of clarity. She knew the critical importance of maintaining crystal clear communication at all times. Both in the Treehouse with her leadership team and then again when coaching Ethan through the steps of crisis response, Sunny made a strong case for the necessity of clarity in any organization.

It's easy to create a sprawling, fifty-page strategic plan. It's hard to boil those fifty pages down to a half page that people can understand, remember, and execute. It's even harder to be willing to be held accountable and evaluated based on the results. The work of clarity is far from easy. From your overall mission and purpose right down to daily tasks and priorities, the more clarity you create, the more trust you will build, and the more positive results you will see.

Clarity unifies, motivates, and boosts morale.

 Consumers report that the #1 way for salespeople to build their trust is to clearly explain the specifics of the product or service, including all costs.
(Trust Edge Leadership Institute, *Trust Outlook*)

Symptoms

Symptoms of weak or compromised clarity include **ambiguity**, **complexity**, and/or **blurring of focus**. Without clarity, sooner or later things will fall apart. Ambiguity in priorities, goals, requests, processes, and deadlines invariably leads to conflict, waste, and delays. Lack of clear distinctions and definitions generates weak performance, failed targets, suspicion, and mistrust.

Whenever you complicate anything beyond what's necessary, you lose clarity, which in turn decreases trust. Think of Ethan's own stumbling block: He thought his biggest strength was to weave vastly complex systems together inside his own head. Meanwhile, his whole team was left in the dark, with no idea where things stood. This often happens, for example, when organizations experience rapid growth and try to build on their success. They let their processes get complex, introduce too many new ideas at once, or promise things to their customers that they cannot deliver on time. They inevitably complicate the original idea that led to their success in the first place!

Clarity is essential not only on the *what* and *when* but also the *why* of a given target or benchmark. Employees are not automatons, they are human beings. People buy in to a project and often work at their best when they are given a clear understanding of the context and overall purpose of a task.

Open, honest communication is the single greatest factor that causes U.S. workers to stay longer with an employer and increase their work performance.
(Trust Edge Leadership Institute, *Trust Outlook*)

Strengthening the Clarity Pillar

Your effort to open the windows of clarity can begin anywhere in the organization where it feels most needed. Because clarity breeds clarity, the more you work toward adding it in any one aspect of the organization, the more transparency and lucidity will result overall.

 Make clear priorities.

Strategic clarity rests on creating and communicating clear priorities. We agree with Jim Collins, who says if you have more than three push-forward priorities, you don't have any at all. Three is maximum, and one is optimum, especially in crisis. Why? Because when it's clear, people can follow it.

One global senior VP of a Fortune 50 company we worked with had far too many priorities. Although he was reluctant at first, we helped him boil his priorities down to three. He later reported that when he started hearing the same priorities coming out of their other offices around the world, he knew he'd gotten it right. "We knew it was working when we started to hear the echo in other parts of the organization," he said. That's the power of clarity.

✔️ Work in ninety-day plans.

An essential part of achieving clear priorities is setting the right time frame. One-year goals are rarely effective; a year out is too far away to keep a clear focus. How long is ideal? It varies. The widespread notion that you can change any habit or behavior in twenty-one days comes from a misreading of the original research, depending on the habit, person, and circumstances. For organizations, we've found the sweet spot is around the top of the curve, or ninety days. It is short enough to stay focused, and long enough to get more done than many people get done in a year.

Once you have your top priority, break that goal down into something your team can achieve within ninety days. You still need to have long-term strategic plans, such as two-year plans or five-year plans, and so forth—but the best way to achieve them is in ninety-day bites.

✔️ Ask the most important question.

Strategic clarity also requires focused action. Once you have a goal and a time frame, what are your team's next steps? Where do you start? At Trust Edge Leadership Institute, we use a rigorous approach based on the most neglected word in business: "How?" You saw Sunny use this approach with her staff, and of course saw how it can go terribly wrong in Ethan's ill-considered first attempt. Be sure that your staff is fully briefed on how the technique is supposed to work!

At Trust Edge, once we've established a clear objective, the first question to ask is, How are we going to do this? Whatever the answer is, we'll ask "How?" again. And then again until we get to a very specific answer. Repeatedly ask the question "How?" as many times as needed until you arrive at a specific concrete action that can be taken today or at the latest, tomorrow. That final "How?" should have a concrete *who*, *when*, and *where* attached to it if needed for clarity. The *who* needs to be a specific individual (not a group or committee), the *when* needs to be a specific time, and the *where* needs to be a specific place. You get the idea. Drill down all the way to the level of real action.

Be sure to use the "How?" exercise on yourself as well! It is just as important for you as an individual to have a clear, immediately actionable goal as it is for your team. If I haven't decided where, when, or how I am going to work out in the morning, I probably won't work out at all!

Drilling down to a specific and actionable goal not only puts you and your team on a path to solid results, it also generates new hope, confidence, and momentum. We call it the How? How? How? process. We've had more than one salesperson attribute it to tripling sales in ninety days. This works. Just ask *"How?"*

 Communicate clear expectations.

People can't do a great job if they don't understand expectations. When I'm specific with my requests, I am much more likely to receive what I asked for. When my requests are vague, the result is likely to be something different than what I had in mind. We use a method for communicating clear expectations called ODC. It stands for outcome, deadline, and clarifiers.

O = *Outcome.* Have I given a specific outcome? Provide as much clarity as possible, including context and purpose, but then let them go be their best.

D = *Deadline.* Have I given a firm, specific deadline for completion? Managers sometimes fear that doing so may lead to conflict—but by not giving a deadline, you ensure conflict. If you say, "I want to see that report soon," they think next week, when you meant tomorrow. They have other deadlines, so it naturally goes to the bottom of the pile.

$C = Clarifiers$. Have I given space for the other person to ask clarifying questions? Am I sure we are on the same page? Is there anything that isn't clear?

More than half of people surveyed said that failing to communicate the reason for a change is what most hinders leaders from building trust.

(Trust Edge Leadership Institute, *Trust Outlook*)

COMPASSION

People put faith in those
who care about others
more than themselves.

CASE 4 TRUST

KICKSTART

CLARITY

COMPASSION

CHARACTER

COMPETENCY

COMMITMENT

CONNECTION

CONTRIBUTION

CONSISTENCY

NEXT STEPS

24
PILLAR 2: COMPASSION

IN OUR GLOBAL SURVEYS we often ask, Who is the most trusted person in the world? By far the single most common answer is "Mom." Why? It's because mothers routinely sacrifice for their children. They are looking out for us. Similarly, why do we trust firefighters, nurses, and teachers? Because by the very nature of their jobs, they care for others, often at their own risk or expense. We trust people who put our interests ahead of their own.

When I first started out speaking at large conferences, I often stood backstage, nervously waiting to go on stage, until my wife leaned in and said, "David, don't think about the research, don't think about your notes. Just love 'em. They can tell when you love 'em." Even today, when I enter the most high-pressure situations, she'll text or call me with the same message: "Just love 'em, David. They can tell when you love 'em." And it's true. People can identify authenticity from a mile away.

Milo was the one who helped Ethan see how The Grove not only treated its staff with compassion, but actually wove compassion into the very organizational policies and structures. Sunny made it a cultural norm to support employees going through personal challenges, and she had instated official policies and programs that helped them with things like housing, health, and family. And of course, Ethan's major breakthrough with 10K was when he reacted powerfully and compassionately to the stress and exhaustion of Zach, the director of software. Instating paternity leave and offering to bring on additional programmers were signals to the team that Ethan was putting his own skin in the game to make a real difference in the well-being of his team.

Compassion in business is more than a purely interpersonal priority. Increasingly, in our interconnected world, it is a global value. Every year, people are finding it harder to trust companies that don't demonstrate they care about society, the environment, the disadvantaged, or the world at large. Show that you genuinely care about others, put their interests first, and you will stand out in your industry.

Symptoms

Symptoms of weak or compromised compassion include *indifference*, *disdain*, and/or *contempt*. You'd think that the opposite of compassion would be cruelty, and in a way this is true. Hatefulness in all its forms—gossip, meanness, pettiness, vindictiveness, discrimination, racism, sexism, ageism, or any other -ism—all clearly point to a lack of caring. Yet the far more common symptom than cruelty is indifference—that is, simply not caring. As psychologists know all too well, neglect is a deeply wounding form of child abuse, in some ways as damaging as more overt expressions of abuse.

In the workplace, a feeling of neglect leads to decreased motivation, poor employee morale, inconsistent performance, and increased rates of attrition—all of which add up to considerable cost. Ethan's big realization was that in his attempt to avoid becoming the micromanager he hated, he had actually abdicated his responsibilities as a leader. Never underestimate the bottom-line impact of compassion—or the lack of it.

Strengthening the Compassion Pillar

Everyone longs to be recognized and appreciated for their hard work. This doesn't mean we should give everyone a blue ribbon. It does mean, though, that when we notice people doing something well and single them out for that, it has an impact. Our global *Trust Outlook* survey found that the number one reason people, of all generations, leave an organization is because they feel unappreciated.

Appreciation can take many forms, some of them unexpected. In our research, we've discovered that people actually crave honest, even critical feedback. People generally want to do a good job, and they want to know how they can improve. If someone you manage is struggling, showing them appreciation can look like an authentic attempt to help them improve. They key is to approach these conversations with compassion. If someone feels that you are in their court and genuinely want to help them improve, they will feel valued and appreciated.

People who feel cared for have a hard time leaving, even for bigger money. Why is that? It's because compassion and care engender loyalty. When a company's leaders care about people, those people come to care more about their colleagues and the company. The great poet Maya Angelou once said, "People will forget what you said, people will forget what you did, but people will never forget how you made them feel."

 Respondents were most likely to leave an organization if they didn't feel appreciated.

(Trust Edge Leadership Institute, *Trust Outlook*)

Practice the LAWS of Compassion.

Four positive habits show you have care and compassion in the home and workplace—listen, appreciate, wake up, and serve others (LAWS).

L = Listen. In our fast-paced, attention span–deprived culture, it's all too easy to become distracted—and bad listening habits aren't just rude, they are expensive. One of the most powerful ways to demonstrate that we genuinely value others is to give them our undivided attention when they speak. That means, we stop, make eye contact, be patiently present, recognize their point of view, and don't give in to interruptions.

A = Appreciate. When you notice someone doing something noteworthy or making a meaningful contribution, say so. Make a habit of pointing out people's intentions, efforts, and meaningful contributions. Although listening to people's needs, expectations, and ideas is important, it's equally important to follow up on what you heard. Taking action and then giving credit to the source is one of the strongest ways to demonstrate your appreciation (see below for more on appreciation).

W = Wake up! Have you ever known someone who can make you feel like you're the only person who matters? While there are people who are born with this quality, it is a skill set everyone can develop. It takes making an effort to stay present, awake, and engaged in the moment.

S = Serve others. It's human nature to prioritize our own goals and well-being. Practicing compassion doesn't mean you have to deny your own interests or become a martyr in all situations, it simply means making a shift in perspective, and developing the habit of looking out for others' interests first. Go the extra mile. Show a generous spirit. Be kind. The more you practice it, the more natural it becomes—compassion is contagious!

Make appreciation specific, personal, and authentic.

It's easy to go through the motions of showing appreciation without having any real impact. To be effective, appreciation needs to be specific, personal, and authentic (I call it the SPA method). In the story, Naomi, director of community at The Grove, uses part of the SPA method when she arranges the special dessert for Ethan and his friends.

S = *Specificity* breeds credibility. Instead of saying "Good job," recognition is a lot more powerful when you can be specific about what the other person achieved.

P = *Personalizing* whenever possible can make a huge difference. Naomi went to the specific trouble of finding out what Ethan's favorite dessert was, rather than just giving him something generic on the house. In an example from my own life, a client once gave me a pair of cufflinks as a gesture of appreciation. What amazed me about them wasn't that they looked expensive or fancy or anything else—it was that they were fly-fishing cufflinks! Somewhere in the course of our work together, this client had learned how much I love fly fishing. It doesn't have to be a gift. A simple note, an observation, remembering their child's name—these are personal gestures that mean a lot.

A = Finally, the appreciation must be *authentic*. Imagine experiencing a terrifying injury on vacation, away from home and your family. Ethan had the Brain Trust around him, but he was stuck in a hotel full of strangers. Imagine how it would feel in that scenario to have a hotel staff member take an authentic interest in your well-being.

Another more sobering example of the power of authenticity comes from a friend of mine. He once told me about a time he developed an incredible system that saved his company enormous amounts of time and money. During the next regular staff meeting, his manager silently slid a little cardboard box over to him. Inside the box was the generic gift the company always used for recognition. My friend says he would have vastly preferred a handshake, a word of appreciation, or a pair of movie tickets to a film someone had thought he might enjoy. He soon left the company and started his own competitive company. What a great cautionary tale!

Making your appreciation personal and specific takes effort, but that effort is worth it. Why? Because it's not the gesture, it's the thought and care behind the gesture that matters most. People love authenticity!

CHARACTER

People respect those
who do what's right
over what's easy.

CASE 4 TRUST

KICKSTART

CLARITY

COMPASSION

CHARACTER

COMPETENCY

COMMITMENT

CONNECTION

CONTRIBUTION

CONSISTENCY

NEXT STEPS

25
PILLAR 3: CHARACTER

IT IS NO SURPRISE that strong character is a necessary
ingredient of trust. This applies to companies as well as individuals. While clarity and compassion have to do with what
you do and how you do it, character cuts to the heart. People
of high character are those who have integrity. They do what
they say they will do. They tend to have a very strong moral
compass. There may be differing views on what makes someone a good person, but most of us, especially within a single
culture, share a fundamental sense of right and wrong. Leaders
of high character tend to do the right thing even when it's the
more difficult path.

   Ethan's conversation about character with Amirah, The
Grove's director of finance, spanned quite a few specific practices, but character is the most subtle of the pillars and can't
be emphasized enough. It can't be measured in the same way
competency can, through metrics, or systematized like clarity.
It has to be fostered through intentional self-reflection, and it
starts with the leader doing an honest assessment of their own
character and choices.

Symptoms

Symptoms of weak or compromised character include *lack of integrity*, *dishonesty*, *divisiveness*, and/or *laziness*. An unusual phenomenon happens sometimes in business. You may find people who are reasonably honest, upright citizens, yet the company they are running descends into all sorts of unethical behavior and even downright dishonesty. Some call this the "mob rule." In the absence of clear leadership by someone of high character, human beings' worst traits can emerge.

Many companies begin with the best of intentions, but when those higher values come into conflict with higher profit, expediency, or other short-term gains, they take the path of least resistance. What dictates whether a company will consistently live up to its own standards is character. We've all seen star athletes, award-winning actors, chart-topping singers, and others shoot to the top of their fields and crash just as fast. There are many reasons for the rise—personality, inborn talent, luck, timing, but just one reason for the crash: a failure of character. You can get to the top on talent; staying there takes character. And the same holds true for companies.

 Almost half of U.S. employees say they would NOT trust their leader at work to hold $5,000 for them!
(Trust Edge Leadership Institute, *Trust Outlook*)

Strengthening the Character Pillar

Establishing strong character within an organization takes conscious effort. A great way to begin is by simply asking yourself the question, "Am I doing the right thing?" and then changing tactics if you think the answer might be "no." The challenge lies in the follow-through and not getting sidetracked by expediency or distraction. The solution? Repeatedly asking that same

CASE 4 TRUST

KICKSTART

CLARITY

COMPASSION

CHARACTER

COMPETENCY

COMMITMENT

CONNECTION

CONTRIBUTION

CONSISTENCY

NEXT STEPS

question: "Am I doing the right thing?" IBM famously rose to dominance with signs on every employee's desk that said: "THINK." For today's companies, I would suggest a sign that says: "DO THE RIGHT THING."

Parents often say, "Have fun!" as their kids go off to an outing. My parents always said, "Be good!" Those are two vastly different messages. It's not that we don't want our children to have fun, but we know that if having fun is their focus, they are more likely to get into trouble. If being good is the focus, they will usually have more fun.

Identify your decision-making values.

One way to increase the likelihood of living with congruent character is identifying a set of specific values that you consult as a behavioral yardstick every time you make a decision of any consequence. I find that a phrase or a few words is often more concrete and tangible than a single abstract word. For example, one of our decision-making values at the Trust Edge Leadership Institute is "excellence in service." Whether we're selecting a venue for an event, making a decision about what countries to include in our next global research survey, or deciding what refreshments to serve at a meeting, we cannot complete that decision without asking, "Does this choice provide our clients with excellence in service?"

The beauty of having a concrete, predetermined set of decision-making values is that it makes your decisions more congruent and consistent, while also faster and easier to decide. To some degree, your decision is already made for you. When you make a decision based on your values, you not only increase your odds for success, you also sleep better at night.

Of course, this works at home too. Years ago, my wife and I came up with a list of qualities we would one day want to see in our grown children, including gratitude, humility, generosity, and so forth. We displayed these values on our dining room table and were able to weave these virtues into a few minutes of casual conversation from time to time. One day when we were considering buying a new car, my wife and I were talking about how much we could get when we traded in our old car. Our young daughter spoke up. "Hey," she said, "one of our family values is generosity. Shouldn't we be giving the car away to someone who needs it?" Our daughter's comment made us stop and reevaluate our decision. It can be effective to both decide and declare your values for all to hear. We did end up donating our car, and it was a tremendous lesson for us all.

Build an organization of character.

High character isn't as easy as the flip of a coin. Character, like trust itself, is something you can intentionally build. We use seven steps to cement high character into the foundation of an organization: define it, communicate it, hire on it, assess it, reward it, discipline it, and systematize it.

1. *Define it.* Character may mean different things to different people. What does character look like in your situation? For the sake of clarity, take some time and define it for your own organization.

2. *Communicate it.* The irony of one of the fallen, most corrupt corporations in American history is that they actually had a strong mission based on some pretty admirable values, but they didn't communicate it, either in word or deed. They didn't speak it, model it, or repeat it, and therefore people didn't follow it. The result was tragic destruction.

3. *Hire on it.* Make character as central to your hiring as skill, training, and prior employment. Warren Buffett's dictum is relevant here: "Hire on character, train on competency."

4. *Assess it.* Ask "How successfully and consistently have I been able to do the right thing?" as a basis for discussion. Whatever review and assessment systems you have in place, make sure

character plays a central role. See www.measuremytrust.com as an option to help you with this.

5. *Reward it.* Some of the client companies we've worked with have made a regular practice of giving out Pillar Awards to employees who exemplify each of the 8 Pillars of Trust. One of the invariable favorites is the Character Award, given to someone showing notably high character.

6. *Discipline it.* When out-of-character incidents occur—stealing, lying, unacceptably poor customer service, and so on—it's critically important to deal with it, and to do so as quickly as possible. Not addressing an issue conveys the message that character is not really that important to you or the company. Managers and leaders sometimes shy away from disciplining poor behavior when the person in question is an otherwise strong performer and they don't want to focus on the negative. This is a mistake. It is crucial to face issues head on, or they will come back to bite you.

7. *Systematize it.* One of the biggest banks in America had a strong, stable reputation throughout the financial crisis of 2007–2009, but that was shattered a decade later when scandal broke over the creation of millions of fraudulent accounts. What made all these branch managers and employees make this choice? An incentive system that pressured them to "cross-sell." Look at the incentive programs you have in place. Are your systems working against the very character you desire?

COMPETENCY

People have confidence
in those who stay fresh,
relevant, and capable.

CASE 4 TRUST

KICKSTART

CLARITY

COMPASSION

CHARACTER

COMPETENCY

COMMITMENT

CONNECTION

CONTRIBUTION

CONSISTENCY

NEXT STEPS

26
PILLAR 4: COMPETENCY

COMPETENCY IS A CRITICAL ELEMENT of trust: We
tend to trust someone who we know can do the job. If you
want your business to establish a strong and lasting foothold in
the marketplace, there is no substitute for a high standard of
competency. This also applies to leadership. What are you doing to stay relevant and capable? In the most recent publication
of *The Trust Outlook,* the number one reason employees gave
for trusting a leader is competency.

Competency is absolutely critical to Bob's job, as director
of safety, at The Grove: to keep staff and guests safe so they can
fully enjoy their time on the mountain. His success in ensuring
everyone on his staff excelled in this pillar was on display when
Milo, just a teenager, was able to quickly immobilize Ethan's
knee, saving him from surgery. However, 10K's major struggles
were not with competency. In fact, it was a pillar where they
excelled. That didn't stop the weaknesses in compassion, clarity, connection, and others from bringing 10K to its knees.

When you visit the dentist, you want to know that he or she knows how to perform a flawless root canal. This is a specific competency. But every field is rapidly evolving and with increasing speed. Specific competency has always been important, but in today's world, continual education and growth is essential to maintaining competency. This is why Bob's competency frameworks were all based around training and development. If you're leading the same way you were twenty years ago, selling the same way you were fifteen years ago, teaching the same way you were ten years ago, then I shouldn't trust you. To be trusted, you have got to stay fresh, relevant, and capable in your area of expertise.

Symptoms

Symptoms of weak or compromised Competency include *lack of discipline*, *complacency*, *arrogance*, and/or *reliance on routine*. Weakness in this pillar manifests itself as complacency and staleness. It's a "This is the way we've always done it" attitude. In an organization that places a high value on competency and capability, there is a vibrancy that comes from the constant striving to do better, to find new ways of delivering excellence at an even higher level. In an organization where the competency pillar is weak, you will find the opposite—a lackluster sense of "good enough" and a resistance to putting in extra time and learning new things.

Beware—this weakened state can come about as a by-product of success. Market leaders often fall into a "rest-on-their-laurels" mentality that keeps them from learning and continuing to grow and develop. When an organization loses that sense of urgency that drove them in the early days, it can be difficult to stay motivated and hungry. The old guard gets entrenched, new ideas are discouraged, and signs of trouble are often ignored. It's a devastating progression. The solution? A renewed focus on excellence, fresh ideas, and continued competency.

Strengthening the Competency Pillar

Competency is the basic reason to hire someone in the first place, but results don't happen simply by hiring competent people. The burning question is, How do we stay competent and capable? How do we ensure that our team members *stay* fresh and relevant?

Consciously building a culture of continuous, lifelong learning is critical. There is a direct correlation between how strongly and consistently a company invests in training its people and steady success. Not only do employees become better and more resourceful performers, but because their place of work becomes a source of personal and professional enrichment, they often become more engaged and committed to the company itself. Trust increases, attrition goes down, and productivity goes up—you are investing in the future!

 Create a plan for continuous learning.

From reading groups to continuing education to the pursuit of advanced degrees, every investment made toward employees' continuous learning is an investment in the company's future. According to *The Trust Outlook*, three in four employees would trust their company more if ongoing training was offered.

 Get involved in mentoring.

Every accomplished leader can point to mentors who played a significant role in their life, career, and success. Often that role has been not just helpful but pivotal. Mentorship is perhaps the oldest and most potent form of training humanity has ever employed. Many different professions had apprentices. Good mentors provide three essential elements: the wisdom of greater experience; a direct, personal commitment to your learning and success; and the willingness to be candid and give honest, constructive feedback.

Establishing a mentorship program at your organization doesn't have to be overwhelming. At a minimum everyone could have and be a mentor, but make it easy. For example, establish that every mentor pair should meet just four times, then have everyone shift. Many mentorship programs fail because they take on too much. Trying to set up a mentor partnership for a year is too long, but this tends to be the length people try start with. Try for something shorter and more sustainable. You will still see massive benefits.

Encourage participation in mastermind groups.

Powerful learning often happens in a group setting. People have an amazing capacity to sharpen one another. This is often displayed in teams where synergy can be harnessed. Continuous learning becomes a team sport when people participate in mastermind groups. At its heart, a mastermind group is typically five or six people who meet regularly to talk over issues, challenges, and goals facing its members. When facing a roadblock, five minds are far more likely to have the answer than one. This practice has had exponential results for me and for my organization. I can't recommend it enough!

76% of all people believe being offered ongoing training would help them trust their employer more.
(Trust Edge Leadership Institute, *Trust Outlook*)

COMMITMENT

People believe in those who
stand through adversity.

CASE 4 TRUST

KICKSTART

CLARITY

COMPASSION

CHARACTER

COMPETENCY

COMMITMENT

CONNECTION

CONTRIBUTION

CONSISTENCY

NEXT STEPS

27
PILLAR 5: COMMITMENT

COMMITMENT IS A VITAL COMPONENT of trust.
Why? Because people trust those who keep their promises and
do not trust those who fail to deliver on their promises. Building a business is never an easy task. It takes passion and hard
work, and no matter how good a job you do, there will always
be unexpected challenges. Yet it is precisely when those challenges arise that the real character of a company is revealed. It's
easy to be compassionate and treat your employees well when
business is booming. However, what happens when a new
competitor suddenly encroaches on your market share and you
find yourself in a crunch?

The greatest leaders in history have been those who
demonstrated an unwillingness to compromise when things
got tough. Because of that, they were able to unite others in
support of their cause. If you think of anyone who has left a
lasting legacy on your life or on history—from a teacher to
Martin Luther King Jr. to Gandhi to Jesus to Joan of Arc—you
will find someone who was trusted and followed because of

their commitment to a cause beyond themselves. Commitment yields devotion and loyalty. The executives and managers who succeed today do so often because they embody a spirit of unwavering commitment.

One of the most valuable assets a business can have is a fiercely loyal customer base. And loyalty is awarded to companies that keep their promises.

Symptoms

Symptoms of weak or compromised commitment include *lack of follow-through*, *disengagement*, and/or *disloyalty*. One of the surest ways to destroy trust is to make promises you cannot keep. This is the danger of exaggerated product benefits, impossible delivery deadlines, and over-the-top claims. When you make promises you cannot possibly keep, you are guaranteeing that you will lose people's trust.

In companies where the commitment pillar is weak, you often see a persistent lack of follow-through. Excellent suggestions not taken, valuable professional insights not acted upon, stated policies not implemented, flavor-of-the-month trainings, and new management buzzwords are all symptoms of compromised commitment.

Recently, I watched the senior leader of a large company addressing a group of the corporation's top five hundred people. In the course of his address, he made a commitment to take a particular action but did not follow through. Following this meeting, our team at Trust Edge Leadership Institute conducted a company-wide survey (our Enterprise Trust Index) and were hardly surprised to find that trust had dropped drastically throughout the company.

 People more than double their chances of accomplishing goals when they have accountability from someone who cares about them.

(Trust Edge Leadership Institute, *Trust Outlook*)

Strengthening the Commitment Pillar

People trust a business that delivers on its promises. I was about to speak before a group of salespeople when the vice president who'd hired me to speak came backstage and said, "Loved your book. Loved that chapter on commitment. Can you go out there and tell my team to be committed to me?" My jaw dropped. Commitment cannot be commanded. It needs to be earned. Before going on stage, I explained to this VP that the best way to get commitment from his team was to find ways to demonstrate his commitment to them. Commitment breeds commitment, and you certainly don't get commitment without giving it. Remember that Milo corrected Ethan's misconception that The Grove is successful because of how loyal the employees are to the company. Instead, Milo explained that what Sunny cares about is how loyal the organization is to the employees.

There's one more part to the story. When that vice president went out on stage himself, he lost his entire team. Why? Because everyone there knew firsthand or could sense his lack of authenticity. Commitment may be expressed in words, but it is demonstrated and experienced only through positive, consistent action.

 Make a habit of commitment in the little things.

When someone says, "I'll get back to you within twenty-four hours" and two days go by without word, you lose trust. Every broken promise erodes trust. We make thousands of promises, often without consciously using the word "promise" or even realizing that's what we're doing. One of the most striking ways you can demonstrate commitment is to start meetings on time—and end them on time.

Get clarity on your commitment.

To maintain your commitment to something, you have to be clear about what it is that you are committed to. Use the following three questions to get clarity on your commitments. These questions can be tweaked for an individual, a team, a department, or the mission of an entire organization:

1.   Who are we?

2.   What do we stand for?

3.   What are we committed to?

 Take responsibility for mistakes.

Trusted leaders never deflect blame onto others. They operate by the dictum "Share successes, own failures." When things happen that cause a breach in promise, large or small, how do you rebuild trust? Start with a sincere apology. But the only way to rebuild trust is through making and keeping a new commitment. If you're late for a meeting or fail to complete a promised deadline, it's fine to say, "Sorry I'm late" or "I'm sorry I didn't get that done on time." However, unless you start reliably, predictably, and consistently showing up on time, the apology will ring hollow. People appreciate the apology but trust the follow-through. Use mistakes as opportunities for renewed commitment.

 Make your commitments public.

A commitment becomes a great deal more powerful when you declare it publicly. Once you do, you're accountable. Now it has teeth. Public commitment builds fans, both among clients and within your own team. Here are a few examples of some well-known public company commitments:

Excellence—Ritz-Carlton Hotel Company
Their employees are committed because they're proud to be part of the prestige of excellence they represent. It brings deeply committed clients and many referrals.

Purpose—Henry Ford Health System

Employees and donors have a strong *why*. Their mission is "to improve people's lives through excellence in the science and art of health care and healing." Their vision is "transforming lives and communities through health and wellness—one person at a time."

Transparency—Zappos

One of their core values is "Build open and honest relationships with communication." Employees and buyers alike appreciate their style.

Meaning—Habitat for Humanity

Employees and volunteers are committed because they care about the vision. They want to see "a world where everyone has a decent place to live."

CASE 4 TRUST

KICKSTART

CLARITY

COMPASSION

CHARACTER

COMPETENCY

COMMITMENT

CONNECTION

CONTRIBUTION

CONSISTENCY

NEXT STEPS

CONNECTION

People want to follow, buy from, and be around friends.

28
PILLAR 6: CONNECTION

AT ITS CORE, trust is about relationships, and relationships are about connection. The surest, most durable way to build a sense of unity and team spirit is by fostering a culture of collaboration and partnership that builds upon individual, person-to-person connections.

In American culture, there is a hero worship of the solo entrepreneur, an ethos that says great things are achieved by the lone woman or man who scales the mountain all by herself or himself, the lone ranger. Ethan echoes the business world at large, where this idea is exemplified by the phrase "It's lonely at the top." But if you're lonely at the top, then you're doing leadership wrong. You need a team. We all need teams. This is not to take away from the importance of leadership, but all great innovations and accomplishments are the result of powerful collaboration. Is it messy? Yes. Is it worth it? Absolutely!

Fostering a greater sense of connection increases speed and accuracy of communication and reduces stress. Workers are more inclined to be kind and understanding, to give each other the benefit of the doubt, which reduces friction and increases creativity, innovation, and productivity. Connection was one of the main pillars that had broken down at 10K. It was Ethan's college buddy J.J. who gave him an answer to "How do I increase connection?" with the Trust Shield exercise he described at the après-ski dinner. That exercise is explained in much more detail below.

Connection is also crucial for growth. I've worked with leadership teams that failed to connect personally, and they were also the teams that had a hard time connecting professionally. Ethan realized that his experience with the Brain Trust contrasts sharply with the relationships at 10K, the relationships between himself and the leadership team, and the team members' relationships with each other. He saw how the Brain Trust's friendship—built of long years sharing dreams, trials, successes, and failures— formed an unbreakable foundation for trust. While Ethan gets practical advice from Sunny, it is within the safety in his relationships with his friends Tripper, Pete, and J.J. where Ethan is able to acknowledge and take responsibility for his genuine failures as a leader. It isn't until we confront the reality of our own situations that we are able to learn, grow, and improve.

Connection is increasingly more fragile in today's world, where the speed of change and digitization of communication can easily create more fractionalization and a deeper sense of isolation. With the enormous recent shift to remote work, connection can be very difficult to foster, yet in the new economy, connecting and collaborating are a necessity.

More than half of American workers say that one-on-one meetings with co-workers and supervisors builds trust faster than any other action.
(Trust Edge Leadership Institute, *Trust Outlook*)

Symptoms

Symptoms of weak or compromised connection include *cliques*, *isolation*, *siloing*, and/or *individualism*. In an environment where interpersonal connection is weak, every problem easily becomes exaggerated. Like families that never eat together, a company that doesn't consciously build a culture of connection starts to come apart at the seams.

This pattern becomes obvious when people are seen protecting their turf, being unwilling to share information or resources, and even climbing over others with a dog-eat-dog competitiveness. Workers become more distrustful of each other and of the company leadership, and this sense of malaise can easily bleed over into relations with suppliers, clients, and customers. By that fateful Thursday morning at 10K, connection had disintegrated so badly that no one in the leadership team had shared crucial information between departments in weeks, and no one had felt secure enough in their relationship with Ethan to let him know the reality of their situation.

The Trust Shield

Dozens of activities can help build a culture of connection—from breakfast get-togethers to weekend retreats. The key in these activities is not the activity per se, but that there is ample opportunity for the people involved to tell their stories. For thousands of years, storytelling has served to form connective tissue within groups. The exercise J.J. describes at dinner is called the Trust Shield, and it is one we do ourselves at the Trust Edge Leadership Institute and with our clients. It's straightforward and incredibly powerful. The image of a shield (see next page), also available as a PDF download on our website, should form the framework for this exercise.

The choice of a shield as imagery wasn't arbitrary. Shields throughout history have been used as a proclamation of personal identity, loyalty, and values. The imagery on the shields carried by soldiers in Rome, medieval knights, and royalty proclaimed the bearer's identity and what they stood for. The family crest is the precursor to the modern logo. When we do trainings internationally, we want to be sure the shield resonates with the specific culture where we are working. Our shield for trainings in Kenya is a different design than the shield design for trainings at home in the United States, for example.

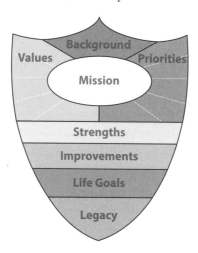

Before you write this off as something resembling glorified kindergarten or summer camp, consider that the Trust Edge Leadership Institute has done this exact exercise with CEOs of billion-dollar companies, college football coaches, and government leaders around the world. In the United States, I've done this with forty members of congress, twenty from one party and twenty from the other. This activity alone changed how they were willing to work with the opposing side, and it directly changed how they acted on the congressional floor.

When you create your own Trust Shield, you are proclaiming your values to share with your colleagues. Sharing Trust Shields is best accomplished in a formal setting, where people are assigned to small groups. Doing the Trust Shield exercise at your organization will give you two big wins:

1. *Individual.* Everyone who creates their own shield will gain greater knowledge and insight into their own life, values, and self. I've worked with CEOs who have done this exercise and realized that they had spent months and thousands of dollars to consider and develop the mission and values of their company without ever having thought about their own personal mission or values. This alone can be transformative.

2. *Organizational.* It should be clear at this point that the Trust Shield will increase and foster connection within a community. But its benefits go even deeper. As J.J. said, the exercise tends to help people humanize each other. Of course it allows a space where people can discover their similarities, but it doesn't end there. I've seen the Trust Shield reveal profound differences that generated just as much and sometimes even more connection and rapport. Ultimately, the Trust Shield increases the willingness of folks to give each other the benefit of the doubt, which opens the door to strong, trusting relationships.

Despite being framed as a shield, something meant to protect you, this exercise instead necessitates vulnerability. But the beautiful paradox of the Trust Shield is that in making yourself more vulnerable, you are actually protecting yourself by building relationships of trust all around you. To create your Trust Shield, reflect on each of these areas and fill in the graphic accordingly. Express yourself however you want—words, pictures, anything that will remind you later of what you have expressed here:

1. *Background.* Think of a few of the most defining moments of your life, the ones that made you who you are today. You don't have write the whole story, but write down some keywords or draw images that represent those moments.

2. *Mission.* What drives you in life? What is your purpose, what are your passions?

3. *Values.* Write up to five of your top values, things like honesty, transparency, or fairness. These values are so important to you, you use them to guide your most important decisions.

4. *Priorities.* What are your biggest priorities? What are the most important dimensions of your life? Family, faith, friends, education, service, and justice are some examples.

5. *Strengths.* What are you good at? Where do you excel? This can be in work or your personal life. What do other people say you are good at? Kick that imposter syndrome to the curb and own your strengths here!

6. *Improvements.* What are you currently seeking to improve about yourself? Challenge yourself to push through any nerves this brings up for you. What one skill, if you could improve it tomorrow, would contribute most directly to your success?

7. *Life goals.* Write a few goals—try to get at least one short-term and one long-term goal that you are currently working toward.

8. *Legacy.* If you disappeared tomorrow, how would you want to be remembered? What legacy do you want to leave behind you when you are gone?

The #1 action that builds trust with a new hire is to meet with them one-on-one in their first week on the job.

(Trust Edge Leadership Institute, *Trust Outlook*)

Strengthening the Connection Pillar

Beyond scheduling specific activities, helpful as they are, the key to rebuilding this pillar is to develop habits and behaviors that foster strong connection in the everyday course of business. For example:

 Meet with people one on one.

In one organization, we discovered that there were all sorts of problems that stemmed from the fact that the branch offices didn't really know anyone at corporate, so even though it was their home office, they didn't trust them. This was a billion-dollar company, and the CEO was an enormously busy woman. However, based on our recommendation, she made a commitment to sit down for lunch with each one of her fifteen branch office leaders once every three months. Traveling to each location took time from fifteen days out of each quarter, an enormous chunk, but she did it. It completely changed the culture. Skepticism, suspicion, second-guessing, whining, and complaining all ceased. Employee satisfaction and productivity skyrocketed.

 Be a little more vulnerable.

Leaders often seek to hide their mistakes and failings out of the belief that if they reveal those parts of themselves, others will respect them less and trust them less. In fact, the opposite is true: The more open and honest you are about your own mistakes, the more people are willing to trust you, protect you, and give you the benefit of the doubt. In fact, our research revealed that 92 percent of employees would trust their senior leaders *more* if they were more transparent about their mistakes!

Emphasize magnetic traits; eliminate repellant traits.

Have you ever noticed that some people walk into a room and light it up? One might assume this ability is innate and exclusive to those who are outgoing and charismatic, but closer inspection tells you that's not the case. One of the most magnetic people I know is an introvert who simply cares about people. She is a great listener and others are drawn to her. She sees the best in others, avoids complaining, asks engaging questions, and focuses on others. Some behaviors automatically draw people to us, while others repel. For example, arrogance and self-importance push people away; expressing a sense of gratitude and appreciation draws people in. Here are a few other examples of magnetic traits versus repellant traits:

Magnetic Traits	vs.	Repellant Traits
grateful	vs.	thankless
listener	vs.	talker
talks about ideas	vs.	talks about others
sees positive side	vs.	constantly complaining
optimistic	vs.	pessimistic
encouraging	vs.	critical
honest	vs.	exaggerating
sincere	vs.	fake
humble	vs.	egotistic
confident	vs.	arrogant
respectful	vs.	sarcastic
vulnerable	vs.	strong

 Ask curious questions.

Few things establish stronger connections with people more than asking them about themselves. We agree with noted author and speaking coach Patricia Fripp, who says, "The key to connection is conversation; the key to conversation is questions. Therefore, learn to ask great questions." And then, we suggest, listen to the answers. The listening is as important as the asking. It is not about prying. The key here is authentically taking an interest in others. Ask yourself, "Who is this person?" and let your genuine interest lead the conversation. Here are some examples to get you started:

- ❑ Who did you look up to most as a child?
- ❑ Who are your heroes?
- ❑ What did you want to be when you grew up?
- ❑ What is your proudest achievement?
- ❑ What are the areas where you need to improve?
- ❑ What do you like to read?
- ❑ What do you most hope for in the future?

Collaboration is the #1 reason Americans persevere on a project.
(Trust Edge Leadership Institute, *Trust Outlook*)

CASE 4 TRUST

KICKSTART

CLARITY

COMPASSION

CHARACTER

COMPETENCY

COMMITMENT

CONTRIBUTION

CONSISTENCY

CONNECTION

NEXT STEPS

CONTRIBUTION

People respond
immediately to results.

29
PILLAR 7: CONTRIBUTION

CONTRIBUTION IS ABOUT delivering results. We trust those who deliver the desired outcomes. It is the ultimate bottom-line measure of an individual's value to the team, and the benchmark of the organization's value to its audience or marketplace. The contribution pillar comes near the end of the list because that is "where the rubber meets the road." You may have excellent character, care deeply about the people you work with, and be 100 percent committed to the team, but in the final analysis that does not matter if you consistently fail to deliver results. Be a caring, committed person of high character—and get things done.

Naomi gives Ethan a crash course on how to encourage contribution when she tells him about the single Difference-Making Action (DMA) that every Grove staff member is trained to identify for themselves each morning. Hand-in-hand with that more concrete tactic is the mind-set shift she references: Most people focus on the action they need to take. But even more powerful is being able to move away from thinking about the action in isolation and instead thinking about the results that action will have over time. The relationship between contribution and trust is self-reinforcing. Consistently delivering results is a sure recipe for gaining trust, and at the same time, working within an environment of higher trust will also lead to greater contribution from all its members.

Symptoms

Symptoms of weak or compromised contribution include *red tape*, *disorganization*, *endless meetings*, and/or *lack of follow-through*. When this pillar is weak, you see the rise of excuses, late or careless work, overwhelmed team members, and poor morale. There is a lack of focus and often unnecessary or unproductive communication, procedures, red tape, redundancy, and waste. Deadlines become unreliable and standards grow shaky. This is the equivalent of a hospital patient's plummeting vital signs, and it indicates that unless you take steps to reverse the decline, the end may be near!

Globally, 72% of people think that Millennials (those who are 38 or younger) generate the most results at work.
(Trust Edge Leadership Institute, *Trust Outlook*)

Strengthening the Contribution Pillar

Two hundred great ideas are worth less than one good idea carried out to completion. Entrepreneurs often face this problem. They may have a big vision but run into trouble figuring out how to follow through on it. This is a major reason many new companies fail. They lack the effectiveness to implement their great ideas. At the same time, contribution doesn't simply mean getting things done. It means getting *the right things* done. An organization with a strong contribution pillar is one that has a bias for action, but specifically for action that makes a significant contribution to fulfilling the organization's mission.

✔ Build a culture of contribution.

Six positive habits can help motivate a results-oriented organization. We call them the Six Es of contribution.

1. *Example.* People do what they see. Actions speak louder than words. Be the first to show up and the last to leave.

2. *Expectation.* People generally step up to the level of performance that is expected of them. Expect great things and you might get them; expect less than great things and you're certain to get them.

3. *Education.* Invest the time and resources to teach people what they need to know to do their job well. Provide the training they need to predictably and consistently deliver results. Learning motivates.

4. *Encouragement.* Nobody gets enough encouragement. Encouragement given sincerely and repeatedly is worth gold.

5. *Empowerment.* Make sure you provide people the resources they need to do their job effectively. Empower the right people for the right jobs publicly.

6. *Extending trust to others.* Nothing supports results like instilling ownership of the task in those responsible for getting it done. Failing to learn how to delegate effectively is the downfall of many an aspiring leader. Extending trust to others can be powerful when done with care and discernment.

Identify Difference-Making Actions (DMAs).
Consistently delivering results requires that you distinguish among the many tasks. Focus on a few DMAs that are central to forward progress. Here are the three steps to implementing DMAs:

1. First thing every morning, write down your most important current goal at the top of a blank page or sticky note.

2. Write the numbers 1 through 5 down the left-hand side.

3. Next to the 1, write the single most important action you can take today to achieve that goal, followed by the next one to four most important things on the other numbered lines. (Write down no more than five tasks.)

As you identify and write down these DMAs, make sure they are focused, clear, and realistic.

☐ *Focused.* There should be no more than five. If you can't boil down your current most important goal to a few simple tasks, you probably need to go back and refocus that goal.

☐ *Clear.* The focus here is actions, not outcomes. You can't control the outcomes, but you can control what *you* are going to do. Make sure each action is concrete and quantified: "Spend two hours on the proposal" rather than "Spend time on the proposal." There must always be a number or explicit time frame attached.

☐ *Realistic.* Your DMAs won't make any difference if you can't actually do them.

Once you have your list of the day's most critical actions, build your day around them. Prioritize them over all other meetings, communications, and other tasks. If possible, have DMAs accomplished by lunchtime, engage them before anything else, then respond to whatever else comes up without it interfering with the most crucial work.

Goal: _____

Today's Difference-Making Actions:

1. _____

2. _____

3. _____

4. _____

5. _____

CASE 4 TRUST

KICKSTART

CLARITY

COMPASSION

CHARACTER

COMPETENCY

COMMITMENT

CONNECTION

CONTRIBUTION

CONSISTENCY

NEXT STEPS

CONSISTENCY

People love to see
the little things
done consistently.

CASE 4 TRUST

KICKSTART

CLARITY

COMPASSION

CHARACTER

COMPETENCY

COMMITMENT

CONNECTION

CONTRIBUTION

CONSISTENCY

NEXT STEPS

30
PILLAR 8: CONSISTENCY

PERHAPS THE MOST IMPORTANT THING to know about trust is that it is never static. Every transaction, every conversation, every encounter matters. Trust either increases or decreases with every interaction. It is this fact that makes trust so powerful and so essential. You can build trust in a moment, with even just one action. But one single inconsistency can change people's perspective. Trust is fragile.

Consistency is the king of the pillars because it has dominion over all the others. Character once in a while is not character. Commitment only when times are good is not commitment. Compassion only to people who look like you is not compassion. If you deliver results sometimes, but not always, other folks will have a hard time trusting you.

There's a reason consistency was the topic of the last conversation Ethan had, and with the oldest member of The Grove's staff. It's a simple concept, but one clear to Eddie, the driver, after many years watching Richard, Richie, and finally Sunny grapple with what makes or breaks the culture of The

Grove. It's the little things, not the big things, done consistently, that make the difference. If I'm overweight, it's because I've had too many scoops of ice cream over the years—not because of what I ate this morning. If I'm a good husband, it's because I've loved and honored my wife over time—not because I once gave her a diamond ring and a dozen roses. If I'm a good leader, it's because I've shared and embodied the company vision every day—not because I shared it at the annual meeting.

Consistency is what builds the strength and trustworthiness of every other pillar.

Symptoms

Symptoms of weak or compromised consistency include *chaos*, *uneven work*, *inconsistent behavior*, and/or *unpredictability*. When consistency is weak, the fabric of the entire business starts to crumble, perhaps rapidly, perhaps slowly, but with the same inevitable result. It is extremely difficult to hang onto market share or a loyal customer base when people cannot be sure of what to expect.

One day in the boardroom of a company, a leader got so angry he threw a clipboard at someone. After that, no one could fully trust him again. Others on the board became afraid to bring him bad news. Because of that one outburst, the people around this leader stopped telling him the truth. That one moment changed the company's fortunes for the worse.

The #1 action that would increase how long Americans stay with an employer is keeping promises!
(Trust Edge Leadership Institute, *Trust Outlook*)

Strengthening the Consistency Pillar

Building consistency doesn't happen by accident; it takes intention and persistent effort. A friend of mine was in a terrible car accident a few years ago and spent five-and-a-half weeks in a coma, and it was over three months before he could stand up. Thankfully, when he finally awoke, there was no brain damage, but his body had badly atrophied. My friend had been a masters-level bodybuilder, with a phenomenal physique, yet over those sixty-six days of inactivity, he'd lost sixty-six pounds.

The lesson? Unless you are actively building trust every day in your business, atrophy will take hold. Consistency is what builds the muscle, the body, the marriage, the reputation, the brand, the health, and the vibrancy of the organization. So how do you build consistency? By putting in place clear frameworks, reliable systems, and regularly communicated values that support the same results across the organization. Atrophy is guaranteed without intentional action.

 Review your brand on a regular basis.

Consistency is what creates an individual's reputation and a company's brand. Ultimately your brand is determined not by slogans or marketing campaigns but by what your business delivers, day in and day out. One excellent way to keep a thumb on the pulse of your organization's consistency pillar is to conduct a brand review every ninety days. Try asking these questions:

❑ Where is my organization most on brand? Where is the brand strong?

❑ Where is my organization most off brand? Where could we benefit most by becoming more consistent?

- ❏ What can I/we do to increase consistency in our brand over the next ninety days?
- ❏ *How* will I/we do that?
- ❏ How *specifically*?
- ❏ How *very* specifically?

 Build consistency by creating positive habits.

Let's face it, even with the best of intentions, positive change is not easy. We all know from personal experience that patterns of behavior don't change on their own! In the face of significant challenges, though, people can change for the better. The key to generating positive change and building consistency is focus and discipline. You can apply this process to a personal habit of your own that you want to change, or to a chronic behavior within your organization.

1. *Write down the habit you want to change.* Consider the consequences of not changing it and the benefits of doing so. Writing it down solidifies the commitment. Detailing costs and benefits clarifies the stakes.

2. *Identify a replacement habit.* It's easier to replace a given habit with a new, more positive habit than to simply attempt to quit the negative habit.

3. *Work on one habit at a time.* Lumping several habits together splits your focus. Keep it simple and laser-focused. Once you've affected this change successfully, you can move on to the next.

4. *Set a target date.* By what day will you have effectively replaced the old habit with the new one?

5. *How* will you make this change?

6. How *specifically*?

7. How *very* specifically?

The Final Problem

You don't trust someone because they say, "Just trust me." You trust someone who earns your trust. This is essentially the problem. Many people we talk to want to have a motivational solution to every problem in five minutes or less. Trust isn't like that. It takes work. Just like the lawn does not mow itself and the laundry does not fold itself, someone has to do the work. It is the same with trust. You have to take your trust-building vitamins and do your trust homework if you want to become an effective leader. It is work, but it is worth it. It is the only way to lasting success and long-term impact.

People ask me about being *trusted* versus being *trustworthy*. The problem is you can manipulate the 8 Pillars of Trust to *appear* trusted for a time without actually being *worthy* of it. What are we really going for? Trustworthiness! People might mistakenly trust a leader, but is the leader worthy of their trust? That is our goal, to be worthy of everyone's trust. And, let me tell you, that takes work every single day. Your friends, family, team, and staff—they need you. The world needs you. It's noble work to become a TRUSTED LEADER, and if you commit to this journey, you are guaranteed to flourish!

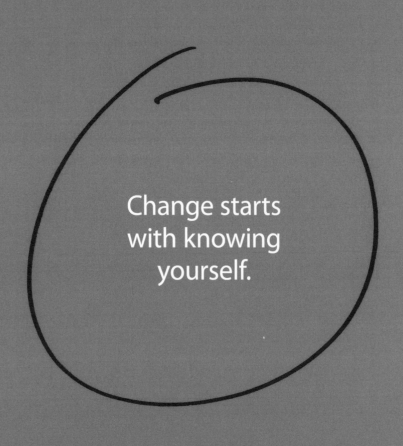

Change starts
with knowing
yourself.

Next Steps

FOR A QUICK OVERVIEW of where you and your organization stand on the 8 Pillars of Trust, take this brief self-assessment.

Yourself

On a scale of 1 to 10, how strongly do people experience each of the pillars in *you* right now?

___ Clarity

___ Compassion

___ Character

___ Competency

___ Commitment

___ Connection

___ Contribution

___ Consistency

Your Organization

On a scale of 1 to 10, how strong is each of the pillars in your business or organization right now?

___ Clarity

___ Compassion

___ Character

___ Competency

___ Commitment

___ Connection

___ Contribution

___ Consistency

For a deeper look in the trust mirror, go to *www.TrustEdge* *.com/assessment*, where you can take a twenty-four question self-assessment. The assessment will offer deeper insights into your own behaviors in relation to the 8 Pillars.

Now What?

Once you've assessed where you stand in relation to all 8 Pillars, what do you do with that information? Be encouraged. Most people fixate on their weakness. Start by celebrating what you are doing well! What is your organization's strongest pillar right now? How about for you? Whatever you're doing there, do more of it!

Next, which pillar holds your greatest opportunity? That is, which of the 8 Pillars is currently weakest? Where can you most immediately and directly build more trust, whether with people within the company or with your suppliers, clientele, customer base, or members?

From this point, ask *How? How? How?* until you have a specific action you will take today or tomorrow at the latest. Continue this process and you will increase trust, the greatest advantage in business and in life!

How You Can Move Forward

1. **Start with a Speaking Event.** The first step is to get everyone on the same page. Inspire a shift of thinking around trust by giving your people actionable tools that they can use right away to increase trust. www.DavidHorsager.com

Enjoy fresh research, engaging stories, clear takeaways, and customized content in keynotes, half-days, or workshops.

2. **Find a Trust Edge Certified Coach.** Bring in an expert to help you build and foster the 8 Pillars of Trust in your organization. www.TrustEdgeCoaching.com

3. **Become a Trust Edge Certified Coach.** Equip yourself or those you lead with actionable resources, ongoing training, and custom support to facilitate lasting change that actually works. www.TrustEdgeCoaching.com

4. **Measure Trust.** Trust Edge Assessments provide a benchmark and a clear path forward so that you can see and close gaps in trust. Our easy-to-use dashboard with analytics makes measuring trust simple and actionable.

These powerful tools include: Self-Assessment, Trusted Teams Assessment, Trusted Customer Assessment, and the Enterprise Trust Index.™ www.MeasureMyTrust.com

5. **Transform Culture.** Create and enjoy a high-performing culture of trust. Custom transformation tracks are available to align with your unique identity and priorities. www.TrustEdge.com

651-340-6555 | Info@TrustEdge.com

THE ANNUAL
TRUST OUTLOOK™

Your people want you to focus on THIS p.4

How to build trust during change p.16

7 keys to leadership development that WORK p.12

SPECIAL REPORT:
Trust in healthcare p.20

Research presented by

TRUST EDGE
LEADERSHIP INSTITUTE

The Research

ALL DATA FEATURED in *Trusted Leader* is from *The Trust Outlook*, an annual research study produced by the Trust Edge Leadership Institute. The goal of each study is to understand the current landscape and future impact of trust by surveying thousands of individuals. Each year, we examine a variety of countries to generate a global perspective and provide practical tools for leaders to increase trust in their organizations. Topics covered range from trust within organizational culture and families to trust in sales and leadership. The study continues to prove the bottom-line impact of trust.

The survey is conducted online, and the total sample has a margin of error averaging ±1.8 percent. Learn more at:

www.TrustOutlook.com

Acknowledgments

To my best friend and wife, Lisa, you inspire me to be a more trusted leader, husband, father, and friend every day.

To my lifelong accountability guys (Joe, Jason, Scott) and mastermind group (Jay, Jason, Rory), massive thanks to you all for your incredible examples of leadership and friendship.

To the entire Trust Edge Leadership Institute team, whose editing and insights made this project better, thank you.

To Ryan Naylor, special thanks for encouraging me to write this book with the hope of even greater reach and impact.

To Anna Leinberger, John David Mann, and Jay Payleitner, sincere gratitude for your help and guidance in developing this parable around trust.

To Heidi Koopman and Heidi Sheard, your remarkable design and editing take our brand to the next level—thank you.

To the whole team at Berrett-Koehler, especially Jeevan and Steve, who believed in this story, thank you for being an amazing partner in bringing this book to the world.

To our clients who have believed in us and championed this work around trust and leadership in your organizations, we owe a huge and sincere THANK YOU!

Index

About the Author

DAVID HORSAGER, MA, CSP, CPAE, is the CEO of Trust Edge Leadership Institute, national bestselling author of *The Trust Edge* and *The Daily Edge*, inventor of the Enterprise Trust Index, and director of one of the nation's foremost trust studies, *The Trust Outlook*. He has advised leaders and delivered life-changing presentations on six continents, with audiences ranging from Delta, FedEx, and Toyota to the New York Yankees and the US Department of Homeland Security. His work has been featured in prominent publications such as *Fast Company*, *Forbes*, and the *Wall Street Journal*. Through speaking, training, consulting, and coaching, David and his team at Trust Edge Leadership Institute make it their mission to develop trusted leaders and organizations. With his trademark 8 Pillar framework, David breaks trust down into tangible steps that individuals and organizations can leverage right away to build a high-trust culture where everyone can perform at their best. One of Horsager's great joys is seeing leaders and cultures transformed by trust. He and his wife, Lisa, and their four children live on a hobby farm in Minnesota. You can read more at www.DavidHorsager.com.

Also by David Horsager

The Daily Edge
Simple Strategies to Increase Efficiency and Make an Impact Every Day

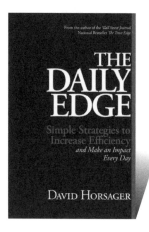

In *The Daily Edge*, you'll learn strategies such as identifying the key Difference-Making Actions on which to focus your efforts. Perhaps it is time to set a personal or even company-wide "power hour" to create time and space to really focus and get things done. The thirty-five high-impact ideas David Horsager introduces in succinct, quick-read chapters are easily implemented and powerful on their own. Taken together, they form a solid wave of efficacy that enables you to get more done, keep your energy up, and make sure that you're able to honor all your relationships, both personal and professional.

Hardcover, ISBN 978-1-62656-595-1
PDF ebook, ISBN 978-1-62656-596-8
ePub ebook, ISBN 978-1-62656-597-5
Digital audio, ISBN 978-1-62656-764-1

Berrett–Koehler Publishers, Inc.
www.bkconnection.com   **800.929.2929**

Berrett–Koehler
Publishers

Berrett-Koehler is an independent publisher dedicated to an ambitious mission: *Connecting people and ideas to create a world that works for all.*

Our publications span many formats, including print, digital, audio, and video. We also offer online resources, training, and gatherings. And we will continue expanding our products and services to advance our mission.

We believe that the solutions to the world's problems will come from all of us, working at all levels: in our society, in our organizations, and in our own lives. Our publications and resources offer pathways to creating a more just, equitable, and sustainable society. They help people make their organizations more humane, democratic, diverse, and effective (and we don't think there's any contradiction there). And they guide people in creating positive change in their own lives and aligning their personal practices with their aspirations for a better world.

And we strive to practice what we preach through what we call "The BK Way." At the core of this approach is *stewardship,* a deep sense of responsibility to administer the company for the benefit of all of our stakeholder groups, including authors, customers, employees, investors, service providers, sales partners, and the communities and environment around us. Everything we do is built around stewardship and our other core values of *quality, partnership, inclusion,* and *sustainability.*

This is why Berrett-Koehler is the first book publishing company to be both a B Corporation (a rigorous certification) and a benefit corporation (a for-profit legal status), which together require us to adhere to the highest standards for corporate, social, and environmental performance. And it is why we have instituted many pioneering practices (which you can learn about at www.bkconnection.com), including the Berrett-Koehler Constitution, the Bill of Rights and Responsibilities for BK Authors, and our unique Author Days.

We are grateful to our readers, authors, and other friends who are supporting our mission. We ask you to share with us examples of how BK publications and resources are making a difference in your lives, organizations, and communities at www.bkconnection.com/impact.

Dear reader,

Thank you for picking up this book and welcome to the worldwide BK community! You're joining a special group of people who have come together to create positive change in their lives, organizations, and communities.

What's BK all about?

Our mission is to connect people and ideas to create a world that works for all.

Why? Our communities, organizations, and lives get bogged down by old paradigms of self-interest, exclusion, hierarchy, and privilege. But we believe that can change. That's why we seek the leading experts on these challenges—and share their actionable ideas with you.

A welcome gift

To help you get started, we'd like to offer you a **free copy** of one of our bestselling ebooks:

www.bkconnection.com/welcome

When you claim your **free ebook**, you'll also be subscribed to our blog.

Our freshest insights

Access the best new tools and ideas for leaders at all levels on our blog at ideas.bkconnection.com.

Sincerely,

Your friends at Berrett-Koehler